STORIES FOR A MAN'S HEART

OTHER BOOKS COMPILED BY ALICE GRAY

Stories for the Heart
More Stories for the Heart
Christmas Stories for the Heart
Stories for the Family's Heart
Stories for a Woman's Heart
Devotions for the Heart (fall 1999)

Keepsakes for the Heart—Mothers
Keepsakes for the Heart—Friendship
Keepsakes for the Heart—Love (summer 1999)
Keepsakes for the Heart—Faith (summer 1999)

(*Keepsakes for the Heart* is an elegant gift collection that includes a hardbound book, complementary bookmark, note cards, and a charming box for keepsakes.)

Stories for a man's Heart

Over 100 Stories to Encourage His Soul

COMPILED BY AL AND ALICE GRAY

Multnomah®Publishers *Sisters, Oregon*

STORIES FOR A MAN'S HEART
published by Multnomah Publishers, Inc.
© 1999 by Alice Gray
International Standard Book Number: 1-57673-480-3

Cover art by Londie G. Padelsky/Index Stock Photography
Design by Stephen Gardner

Printed in the United States of America

Multnomah is a trademark of Multnomah Publishers, Inc.,
and is registered in the U.S. Patent and Trademark Office.
The colophon is a trademark of Multnomah Publishers, Inc.

Library of Congress Cataloging–in–Publication Data
Stories for a man's heart/compiled by Al and Alice Gray.
    p.cm.
    Includes bibliographical references.
    ISBN 1-57673-479-X (alk. paper)
    1. Christian men–Religious life–Anecdotes. 2. Christian men–Conduct of
life–Anecdotes. I. Gray, Al. II. Gray, Alice, 1939–
BV4528.2.S76   1999   99-12520
242'.642–dc21   CIP

99 00 01 02 03 04 05 — 10 9 8 7 6 5 4 3 2 1

TO

BOB AND JAMES

MEN WHO ARE WONDERFUL SONS

AND DEAR FRIENDS—

To our readers—

There are more than 100 new stories in this book,

and we added a few of our favorites from

other books in the "Stories for the Heart" series.

We felt a collection for men would be incomplete without

these extra classic stories. Enjoy!

A SPECIAL THANK-YOU—

To Kerri Loesche and Shawna lynn Shuck

for valuable input and organization of all the paperwork.

To Casandra Lindell, Brad Shuck, and Marty Wilkins

for helping us choose the very best stories.

To the authors for writing stories that

celebrate the honor of manhood.

CONTENTS

VIRTUE—13

LOVE—51

VIRTUE

When God measures a man,
He puts the tape around the heart
instead of the head.

AUTHOR UNKNOWN

THE STUDENT'S MITE

DAVID R. COLLINS
FROM *TEACHERS IN FOCUS*

The situation seemed hopeless.

From the first day he entered my seventh-grade classroom, Willard P. Franklin had existed in his own world, shutting out his classmates and me, his teacher. My attempts at establishing a friendly relationship were met with complete indifference. Even a "Good morning, Willard" received only an inaudible grunt. His classmates fared no better. Willard was strictly a loner, finding no desire or need to lower the barrier of silence he had erected. His clothes were clean—but definitely not on the cutting edge of style. He could have been a trend setter because his outfits possessed a "hand-me-down" look before such a look was in.

Shortly after the Thanksgiving holidays, we received an announcement regarding the annual Christmas collection.

"Christmas is a season of giving," I told my students. "There are a few students in the school who might not have a happy holiday season. By contributing to our Christmas collection, you will help to buy food, clothing and toys for these needy people. You may bring your money tomorrow."

When I called for the contributions the next day, I discovered everyone had forgotten—everyone except Willard P. Franklin. The boy dug deep into his pants pockets as he strolled up to my desk. Carefully he dropped a nickel into the small container.

"I don't need no milk for lunch," he mumbled. For a moment, just a moment, he smiled. I watched him turn and walk back to his desk.

That night, after school, I took our meager contribution—one lone nickel—to the school principal. I couldn't help telling him the giver's identity and sharing with him the incident.

"I may be wrong, but I believe Willard may be ready to become a part of the world around him," I told the principal.

"Yes, I believe it sounds hopeful," he nodded. "And I have a hunch we might profit from him letting us share a bit of his world. I just received a list of the poor families of our school who most need help through the Christmas collection. Here, look at it."

And as I gazed down to read, I discovered Willard P. Franklin and his family were the top names on the list.

My great concern is not whether God is on our side,
my great concern is to be on God's side.

ABRAHAM LINCOLN

BY THE WAY, MY NAME IS JOE

AUTHOR UNKNOWN

He was driving home one evening on a two-lane country road. Ever since the Levi's factory closed, he'd been unemployed, but he'd never quit looking. Now with winter raging, the chill had finally hit home.

It was a lonely road. He could go down this road blind and tell you what was on either side, and with his headlights not working, that came in handy. It was getting dark and the snow flurries had started.

He almost didn't see the old lady stranded on the side of the road. He could see she needed help. So he pulled his sputtering old car up in front of her Mercedes and got out. Even with the smile on his face, she was worried. No one had stopped to help for the last hour. Was he going to hurt her? He didn't look safe—he looked poor and hungry. He could see that she was frightened and cold. He knew how she felt. He said, "I'm here to help you, ma'am. Why don't you wait in my car where it's warm? By the way, my name is Joe."

Well, all she had was a flat tire, but for an older lady, that was bad enough. Joe skinned his knuckles a time or two setting up the jack. His bare hands were so cold he didn't feel it. Soon the tire was changed. As he put the jack away in the trunk, she came back to her car, warmed and calmed. She told Joe that she was from St. Louis and was on her way home. She thanked him and asked how much she owed him. Joe just smiled as he closed the trunk.

Any amount would have been all right with her. She had already imagined all the awful things that could have happened had he not stopped. Joe never thought twice about the money. This was not a job to him. This was helping someone in need and God knows there were plenty who had given him a hand in the past. He had lived his whole life that way and it never occurred to him to act any other way. He told her that if she really wanted to pay him back, the next time she saw someone who needed help, she could give that person the assistance that they needed, and Joe added, "...and think of me."

A few miles down the road the lady saw a small cafe. She went in to grab a bite to eat and take the chill off before making the last part of her trip. It was a dingy looking place. Outside were two old gas pumps. Neither the cash register or the telephone rang very often.

The waitress brought her a clean towel to wipe the snow from her head and face. She had a sweet smile even after being on her feet all day. And she was eight months pregnant, but she never let the strain change her attitude. The old lady wondered how someone who had so little could be so giving to a stranger. Then she remembered Joe.

After the lady finished her meal, and the waitress went to get her change from the hundred dollar bill, she slipped right out the door. When the waitress returned to the table she noticed something written on the napkin. It said, "You don't owe me a thing. I've been there too. Someone once helped me out the way I'm helping you. If you want to pay me back, here's what you do. Don't let the chain of love end with you."

Well, that night when the waitress got home from work and climbed into bed, she thought about the money and what the lady had written. How could she have known how much she and her husband needed it? With the baby due next month, it was going to be hard. She knew how worried her husband was, and as he lay sleeping next to her, she gave him a soft kiss and whispered soft and low, "Everything's gonna be all right. I love you, Joe."

LESSONS FROM A WALLET

BRUCE McIVER

FROM *STORIES I COULDN'T TELL WHILE I WAS A PASTOR*

When I arrived back home in North Carolina after Dad's fatal heart attack, I found his well-worn wallet. In it were some identification cards and six crisp fifty dollar bills. There were no credit cards.

"Mother," I asked, "what are all these new bills doing in Dad's wallet?"

"He knew you and your family were planning to come home in a couple of weeks for your vacation, and he wanted to have some cash on hand so you wouldn't have to spend any of your money while you're here."

I smiled through tears. I should have known, for that was the way Dad was, and it's taken me most of my life to figure it out.

George Sylvester McIver was born in a log cabin near Bear Creek, North Carolina. He and mother left the farm shortly after they were married and made the journey seven miles west to the thriving small town of Siler City. Dad went to work in a furniture factory and lived by the factory whistle for forty-five years. He never made a lot of money by today's standards, but money was never an issue that was discussed around our house.

Except once.

"Ollie," he said to my mother when he came home from work, "I stopped at the grocery store and picked up the items you said we needed. This sack of groceries cost two dollars and sixty-eight cents! We've simply got to cut back on what we buy."

As a seven-year-old boy, I watched and listened in disbelief. Wow! Two dollars and sixty-eight cents—enough to buy just about anything a fellow could ever want.

Looking back, there were times when Dad made two dollars a day in wages, but we had plenty—and more. We lived in a white bungalow that he and Mother had helped build with their own hands. Late at night she would hold the kerosene lamp and Dad would hammer together the finishing touches of the ceiling. We grew our vegetables, milked the cow, churned the butter, raised and killed two hogs a year, made preserves out of blackberries and watermelon rinds, and had fried chicken straight from the backyard any time we desired. My clothing, if inexpensive, was warm and comfortable; and my own mattress, filled with straw or feathers, provided all the luxury a growing boy could hope for as he lay down to sleep.

There was usually a nickel for chocolate candy at Rose's Five-and-Ten-Cents Store, or a double-dip cone of ice cream at Ed Kidd's Sandwich Shop. A dime could always be found somewhere for a western picture show at the Elder Theater on Saturday afternoon, and Dad always came through with fifteen cents for a Friday night basketball game. Sometimes he gave me a quarter, which meant I could have a cold soft drink and some popcorn.

And more.

When I was nine years of age, I was stricken with osteomyelitis, an infection and inflammation of the bone. Three major surgeries were performed on my hip at Duke Medical Center where I was a patient for sixty-nine days. The cost of the surgeries and the hospitalization were never mentioned in my presence. Several years later, after I had my own family and became more aware of medical expenses, I asked Dad how in the world he managed all the bills while I was sick.

"Oh, it wasn't that bad," he replied. "We managed without any difficulty." And, with those words, the conversation about the costs of my surgeries and hospitalizations was ended.

Years later, after he died and after I found his wallet, Mother and I were driving around Siler City, basking in memories and reliving warm experiences. I turned a corner, drove up a street, and passed a house that looked familiar.

"Mother, didn't Dad used to own that house?"

"Yes, he owned it once."

And then, almost without thinking, she added, "I believe that's the house he sold to pay your hospital bills."

Tears welled up in my eyes—tears of gratitude. It took forty-two years to get the answer to my question. And I should have known it all along, for that's the way Dad lived...and died.

The crisp fifty dollar bills found in his wallet said it all.

He knew we were coming home.

WHERE HE STANDS...

*The ultimate measure of a man
is not where he stands in moments
of comfort and convenience,
but where he stands at times of
challenge and controversy.*

MARTIN LUTHER KING

GETTING RID OF THINGS

PHILIP GULLEY

FROM *HOME TOWN TALES*

A big problem we face today is the increasing difficulty of getting rid of things we neither need nor want. For years I've been trying to throw away one dozen half-empty paint cans. I tried setting them out with the trash, but the garbage man wouldn't take them. He said a half-empty paint can is considered toxic waste. They don't want it in a landfill, but it's all right down in my basement next to my children's playroom. I'm grateful our government is doing all it can to keep our dumps clean.

I have a farmer friend who wanted to get rid of an old toilet. The trash man wouldn't take it, either. My friend had just bought a new TV. He put the toilet in the TV box, loaded it in his truck, and drove to the shopping mall in the city. He went inside for half an hour, and when he came out, the TV box was gone and the toilet with it. I thought maybe I'd try that with my paint cans.

When I inherited my grandpa's woodworking bench, I had to get rid of my old bench. Once a month we have heavy-trash pickup in our neighborhood. Theoretically, you can set out any large item, and the trash man will haul it away. I dragged the workbench up out of the basement and carried it to the curb. I thought as long as it was heavy-trash pickup day,

I'd set out some other things. When I came back to the curb with more junk, a woman was standing next to the workbench. She had a protective grasp on it, as if she was afraid someone would happen down the road and wrestle it from her.

"Are you going to take my workbench?" I asked.

"Sure am," she answered. "My husband's gone to fetch the truck."

"I have a table with a broken leg down in the basement. Would you like that, too?" I asked.

"We'll take anything," she said.

"Anything?" I asked. "Even paint?"

"Sure, we'll take paint."

I didn't tell her it was toxic waste.

Once you start getting rid of things, it's hard to stop. Lately we've had too many distant relatives and traveling preachers spending the night at our house. We got to thinking that if folks had to sleep on our couch, they'd stay home and sleep in their own beds. We called the Salvation Army, and they hauled away the furniture in our guest bedroom. I wish we'd thought of that ten years ago.

I had a bicycle that I had to ride all scrunched down. I didn't mind that when I was younger, but now it hurts my back. I tried for a year to get rid of that bike, but everyone I asked already had a bicycle. My brother finally agreed to take it off my hands for fifty dollars. I took the bike by his house and told him I'd pay him just as soon as I got the money.

The things I want most to be rid of are the hardest to dispose. For the past ten years, I've been the unhappy owner of a fiery temper. I am most likely to explode when faced with a household repair. I suspect some of these murder sprees we hear about on the news probably started with a leaky faucet. Whenever I have to fix something around the house, Joan takes the boys and doesn't come back until I'm finished yelling. This nasty little trait is not something I am proud of, and if I could find someone to take it off my hands, I would surrender it gladly. But nobody wants to take our faults from us. Everyone has enough of his own. It's just like bicycles.

When the apostle Paul wrote about the fruit of the Spirit, the last one he included was self-control. "Love, joy, peace, patience, kindness, goodness, faithfulness, gentleness, and, oh yes, one more: self-control." I do pretty well until that last one. I wish Paul had quit while I was ahead.

In the fifth chapter of Galatians Paul said that folks who storm around mad won't inherit the kingdom of God. At the rate I'm going, the only thing I stand to inherit is Grandpa's workbench.

Lots of things I need to get rid of in my life, things that clutter my soul and squeeze out God. And I don't mean old paint and broken tables. I'm talking about anger so toxic it eats away at the soul. I'm grateful God has the last word in these matters, that he meets my failure with forgiveness, my temper with tenderness.

The question should never be who is right,
but what is right.

GLEN GARDNER

ARTHUR BERRY'S ANSWER

DALE GALLOWAY

FROM *HOW TO FEEL LIKE A SOMEBODY AGAIN*

Arthur Berry was a very famous jewel thief who practiced his trade back in the roaring 20s. He was a very unusual thief in that he would only steal from the very rich. Not only did they have to be rich, but they had to be of the elite rich. The story goes that Arthur would pass up many jewels and take only the finest, most precious. He was one thief that was a connoisseur of art. Since Arthur Berry stole only from the highest elite of society it became something of a social status to have been robbed by this notorious robber. This kind of widespread popularity gave the police nightmares.

Well, one day Arthur stole one too many times because the police caught him in the act, and he was shot. While he was suffering excruciating pain he promised himself that he would never steal again. Now, that was a good beginning; but, for some strange happening, Arthur escaped his imprisonment and spent three more years on the loose. Then came his downfall, when an insanely jealous woman turned on him by telling the police where he was. He was recaptured and spent the next eighteen years behind bars. While in prison, Arthur made up his mind that crime didn't pay and that he would never steal again.

When Arthur got out of prison he made his way to a little town up in

New England and settled down. People did not suspect that he was a famous jewel thief, and due to his hard work and neighborliness, he soon became one of the small town's respected citizens.

All went well with Arthur until someone came to the little town and recognized him as the famous jewel thief. As the news spread as to who he was, reporters came rushing in from the largest city newspapers to interview this reformed criminal. One of the questions that was put to Arthur by a young reporter was this one: "Arthur, we know that you have taken from some of the wealthiest people in the world. Do you remember who it was that you stole the most from?" Without a moment's hesitation Arthur answered, "The person that I stole the most from was Arthur Berry. I could have made a contribution to society. I could have been a stock broker. I could have been a teacher. I could have been a successful businessman. I could have done all of these, but instead I spent two-thirds of my adult life in prison. I have spent a lifetime robbing myself."

IT'S A START

GARY SMALLEY AND JOHN TRENT
FROM *LEAVING THE LIGHT ON*

We know a wealthy couple in Dallas who have really struggled with teaching their children servanthood. For one thing, the kids have had almost whatever they've wanted for years. They've become so accustomed to others meeting their needs that the idea of "serving" sounded like something from the Middle Ages...or Mars.

The father in that family realized he was getting a late start, but hey, it was better than no start at all!

A week or so before the holidays, he said to his family, "We're going to do something different this Thanksgiving."

His teenagers sat up and listened. Usually when he said things like that it meant something exotic. Like para-sailing in the Bahamas.

But not this time. "We're going to go down to the mission," he told them, "and we're going to serve Thanksgiving dinner to some poor and homeless people."

"We're going to what?"

"Come on, Dad, you're kidding...aren't you? Tell us you're kidding."

He wasn't. They went along with it because of his firm insistence, but no one was happy about it. For some reason their dad had "gotten weird" and apparently it was something he just had to get out of his system.

Serving at the mission! What if their friends heard about it?

No one could have predicted what happened that day. And no one in the family could remember when they had had a better time together. They hustled around the kitchen, dished up turkey and dressing, sliced pumpkin pie and refilled countless coffee cups. They clowned around with the little kids and listened to old folks tell stories of Thanksgivings long ago and far away.

The dad in the family was thoroughly pleased (would you believe stunned?) by the way his kids responded. But nothing could have prepared him for their request a few weeks later.

"Dad...we want to go back to the mission and serve Christmas dinner!"

And they did. As the kids hoped, they met some of the same people they'd become acquainted with at Thanksgiving. One needy family in particular had been on their minds, and they all lit up when they saw them back in the chow line again. Since that time, the family has had several contacts. The pampered teenagers have rolled up their sleeves more than once to serve the families from one of Dallas's poorer neighborhoods.

There was a marked but subtle change in that home. The kids didn't seem to be taking things for granted anymore. Their parents found them more serious...more responsible. Yes, it was a late start. But it was a start.

IS IT THE TRUTH?

LESLIE E. DUNCAN

FROM *HOMELIFE* MAGAZINE

I shall never forget that short question my father asked me as soon as we were alone in his study. His eyes were watching me closely. They were searching eyes rather than sharp, condemning ones. He was looking for the truth from his son, who had done something seriously wrong. If he had heard what I'd done, he would punish me for it.

I puzzled to myself for a brief moment whether I should deny having done it and trust to luck that he would believe me rather than the other people or should I come right out with the truth.

"Is it true?" he repeated.

I detected appealing love in the tone of his voice rather than sharp condemnation. He was talking to me as man-to-man though we were quite different in our ages. I blinked my eyes hesitantly for only a split second more.

"Yes, Dad!" I almost smiled in reply from the relief it was to me. "It is true! I did it!"

I did not have long to wait to know what he was going to do about the wrong. How much he wanted us children to grow up to be fine Christian people! I was breathing more easily already, but the uncertainty had not been cleared yet.

"Son," he began, as his right hand was extended toward mine and his left hand was placed on my shoulder, "I'm proud of you!"

The tears that welled up in his eyes assured me he meant every word of what he said. I wondered at first what it all meant. Here I had done what I had known was against my father's wishes. He had heard about it, and I had acknowledged my guilt. Then he declared he was proud of me. That did not sound like my minister father.

"I'm proud of you," he repeated and explained, "to know you had the courage to tell the truth, even though you thought you would be punished for what you'd done."

My eyes opened wider. I was seeing something I hadn't noticed so clearly before. For one thing, I saw what stood well to the front—if not clear out ahead of everything else—in my father's estimation. Through the eyes of his thoughts I was seeing too a new idea of character values. "Is it true?" had a greater importance than a demanding, "What have you done?"

He explained in more detail that he wanted us to tell the truth at all times, no matter what it might cost us. He assured me that so far as punishment was concerned, he would punish us more for telling an untruth to cover something wrong than for telling the truth.

I felt better at once when I told the truth. I could think more clearly about the problem waiting to be solved. Dad had not taken care of that for the two of us. I wondered what to expect next. I certainly had been surprised. I saw everything differently.

"I want you to tell me the truth now," he continued, "the way you just did in such a fine way."

"What?" I asked, a bit puzzled.

He wanted to know if I thought I had done what was right. I was in no mood at all to deny this. Why should I? I told the truth before, so I would do it now too. I assured him I was sure I had done wrong and that I should not have done it.

"What do you think you should do to let people know, especially those you have not done right to, that you are sorry and will not do it again?" he asked.

I was busy thinking. Finally I thought of how I could let them know I was really sorry. In addition to that I knew how I could undo some of what had been done; I could remove some of the damage.

"One more thing, Son," smiled Dad with increasing pride.

I wondered what else he could think of before I would leave his study. So much had happened already in our talk together.

"How are you going to make sure you will remember not to do it the next time?" he questioned. "That is what punishment is for—to make us really sorry for what we have done and to be sure we will remember not to do it again."

I outlined roughly what I thought would be suitable for this. He listened closely.

"Since you had the courage to tell the truth," he suggested, "how would this suit you?" He modified the punishment I had suggested for myself. He was not excusing me from the guilt of doing something quite wrong. He was rewarding me in a wise way for being completely truthful about it.

"Before we leave the room," he concluded, "let's kneel right here and tell God all about what has happened. We can ask Him to help us so that we will not make the same or similar mistake again. God knows the pleasant truth is much better than any unpleasant truth. He can help us so that we will always have the pleasant truth from our daily thoughts and actions."

On our knees together, my wonderful father had one of his informal prayer talks with God about our situation—not just mine. I asked God in my childlike way for forgiveness for what I had done and for strength to avoid doing it again.

From that day to the time of his death many years later, I never was afraid to tell my father the whole truth. In fact, I thought so much of him and his respect for the truth that I was always ashamed not to tell him the truth—every bit of it.

RUNNING LATE

BRENNAN MANNING
FROM *THE SIGNATURE OF JESUS*

Several years ago a group of five computer salesmen went from Milwaukee to Chicago for a regional sales convention. All were married and each assured his wife he would return home in ample time for dinner.

The sales meeting ran late and the five scurried out of the building and ran toward the train station. A whistle blew, signaling the imminent departure of the train. As the salesmen raced through the terminal, one of them inadvertently kicked over a slender table on which rested a basket of apples. A ten-year-old boy was selling apples to pay for his books and clothes for school. With a sigh of relief, the five clambered aboard the train, but the last felt a twinge of compassion for the boy whose apple stand had been overturned.

He asked one of the group to call his wife and tell her he would be a couple of hours late. He returned to the terminal and later remarked that he was glad he did. The ten-year-old boy was blind. The salesman saw the apples scattered all over the floor. As he gathered them up, he noticed that several were bruised or split. Reaching into his pocket, he said to the boy, "Here's twenty dollars for the apples we damaged. I hope we didn't spoil your day. God bless you."

As the salesman started to walk away, the blind boy called after him and asked, "Are you Jesus?"

THE TEST

One day, four high school students decided to cut their morning classes. After lunch, they reported to their teacher that their car had had a flat tire. The teacher simply smiled and said, "Well, you missed the test this morning, so take your seats and get out your notebooks."

Still smiling, she waited for them to settle down. Then she said, "First question. Which tire was flat?"

ED AGRESTA

FROM *DON'T COUNT THE DAYS, MAKE THE DAYS COUNT*

LEARNING FROM A
MOTHER'S TENDERNESS

CHARLES SWINDOLL

FROM *GROWING WISE IN FAMILY LIFE*

Dads, let's face it. Most of us learn tenderness from our children's mother. Boys and girls, likewise, learn tenderness from their mothers. Isn't it interesting that if we had a chance to state what we learned from which parent, most of us would say we learned tenderness from our mother and diligence from our dad. From dad we discovered the value of a dollar, the necessity of hard work, the significance of honesty, the importance of standing alone when everything or everyone seems to turn against us; but we learned transparent tenderness from our mother.

Something happened in our family several years ago that reminds me of the value of a tender mother. Cynthia and I had gone to our church on a Friday evening to attend a parents' appreciation banquet, sponsored by the high schoolers. It was well publicized, and the room was packed with parents who came to be appreciated for a change!

Just after the prayer had been offered for the meal, Cynthia got a little tap on her shoulder and one of those serving leaned over and whispered, "Your two younger children are at the door and want to see you." She went and conversed for a moment and then returned to the table, looking rather serious. She picked up her purse and got ready to leave to take care of some need at home. Without knowing all the details about the need, I said, "For a change, honey, why don't you just sit down and enjoy the banquet. I'll go instead. You're always the one who has to give…who gets up in the night…always the one giving up. For a change, let me. Please, sit down."

After hesitating to calm her mother's heart, she sat back down.

I left, not knowing exactly what had happened. At the door I found two tearstained children with tiny red spots on their clothing. Lifting their bikes into the back of our station wagon, I heard the story. Chuck, our nine-year-old, had wanted a little canary very, very badly. We discussed it. Like a good father, I checked the price, and told him we would have to talk about this investment for a while longer.

He worked with us, we worked with him, and we came up with enough to buy the canary and the cage. He loved this little canary. He named it Twit. He would talk with this little bird and feed it regularly. In return Twit chirped and sang and won its way into the heart of our family. Its presence added to the fun in the upstairs part of our home.

Within the last few days, Chuck had creatively strung some little string perches across the cage—in fact, he had gotten a little carried away and put perches all over the inside of the cage. Cynthia had told him, "You need to clip those off and give the bird more room." Well…in the process of cutting the strings, the little bird fluttered too close to the scissors and, much to his surprise, Chuck clipped the bird's toe. The bird began to bleed. Neither Chuck nor Colleen knew what to do. Desperately, he attempted to calm the frightened creature by reaching into its cage to cradle it, thinking that somehow it would live if he could hold it. Suddenly, the bird flew out of his cage into the bathroom and fluttered around the room in a flying frenzy. Within less than a minute it gasped and fell to the floor—dead.

Our two children stared in disbelief. Horrified and alone, they simply did not know what to do. Tiny dots of blood were sprinkled on the bathroom wall and on them…and worst of all, the delightful pet was gone. They rode their bikes to the church to ask for help. When I arrived home with them, I picked up the little bird, wrapped it in tissue and went outside. We found a shovel and dug a deep hole. And with tearstained eyes, we placed that little bird in the ground and pushed the dirt over it.

Without a word, Chuck left my side. He found a small branch on the ground in the backyard, broke it in two, and made a little cross with some Elmer's glue. Then he got a piece of paper and with his own hand he drew little hearts all over the paper. In the middle of it he wrote, "Chuck's Beloved Bird." With tenderness, he took that little message and placed it at the foot of the cross. The three of us knelt there, arm in arm, and prayed. And, yes, we wept.

HONOR

*No person was ever honored
for what he received.
Honor has been the reward
for what he gave.*

CALVIN COOLIDGE

ASKING FOR
FORGIVENESS

LUIS PALAU

FROM *CALLING AMERICA AND THE NATIONS TO CHRIST*

When I returned from a trip overseas, I sensed that something was wrong between Keith, one of our twins and me. So I asked him, "Keith, have I done anything that really hurt your feelings?"

Instantly, he said, "Yes. Last Christmas you promised me a special toy that I really wanted and you never gave it to me."

The fact is that I'd completely forgotten about it. I probed further: "Is there anything else I've done that I've never asked for your forgiveness?"

Again, his answer was immediate: "Remember when Mom said you had to go to the hospital because Stephen was going to be born? You left us at home and took off in a hurry. Remember?" I did.

"Well, you took off and forgot the suitcase with all the stuff." I couldn't believe all the details he remembered! "After you left Mom at the hospital, you came back and you were huffy. When you got here, the suitcase had been opened and everything was thrown all over the place. And you punished me."

My heart sank. "And you didn't do it?" I asked.

"No, I didn't."

I felt terrible. I hugged Keith and asked him to forgive me. There was an instant improvement in our relationship after that. But his honesty made me think of our other son, Kevin. After all, maybe I'd hurt him, too. I went to find Kevin and I asked him the same question: "Have I ever done something wrong and never asked your forgiveness or promised you something and never kept my promise?"

Kevin's answer was as instant as his brother's had been: "Last Christmas you promised us a special toy and you never bought it for us." Kevin had no idea I'd just talked to Keith about the same thing.

Though it was way past Christmas, I took my two sons to the store that day and bought them what I had promised. The important thing wasn't the toy that was all the rage at the time. Obviously, it was a big deal to my boys even if it wasn't to me. The problem was I'd made a promise all too lightly and dropped the ball as their father.

At times, trying to fulfill all my obligations and responsibilities as a husband and father and an evangelist seem impossible. So often, an excruciating schedule lies before me, and sometimes I'm gone from home for weeks at a time. But I listened to my sons and I learned that keeping my word is one of the most important things I can do—no matter what my schedule is.

THREE RED MARBLES

AUTHOR UNKNOWN

During the waning years of the Depression in a small south-eastern Idaho community, I used to stop by Brother Miller's roadside stand for farm-fresh produce as the season made it available. Food and money were still extremely scarce and bartering was used, extensively.

One particular day Brother Miller was bagging some early potatoes for me. I noticed a small boy, delicate of bone and feature, ragged but clean, hungrily appraising a basket of freshly picked green peas. I paid for my potatoes but was also drawn to the display of fresh green peas. I am a pushover for creamed peas and new potatoes. Pondering the peas I couldn't help overhearing the conversation between Brother Miller and the ragged boy next to me.

"Hello, Barry, how are you today?"

"H'lo, Mr. Miller. Fine, thank ya. Jus' admirin' them peas—sure look good."

"They are good, Barry. How's your ma?"

"Fine. Gettin' stronger alla time."

"Good. Anything I can help you with?"

"No, sir. Jus' admirin' them peas."

"Would you like some to take home?"

"No, sir. Got nuthin' to pay for 'em with."

"Well, what have you to trade me for some of those peas?"

"All I got's my prize aggie—best taw around here."

"Is that right? Let me see it."

"Here 'tis. She's a dandy."

"I can see that. Hmmmm, only thing is this one is blue and I sort of go for red. Do you have a red one like this at home?"

"Not 'zackly—but, almost."

"Tell you what. Take this sack of peas home with you and next trip this way let me look at that red taw."

"Sure will. Thanks, Mr. Miller."

Mrs. Miller, who had been standing nearby, came over to help me. With a smile she said: "There are two other boys like him in our community— all three are in very poor circumstances. Jim just loves to bargain with them for peas, apples, tomatoes, or whatever. When they come back with their red marbles, and they always do, he decides he doesn't like red after all and he sends them home with a bag of produce for a green marble or an orange one, perhaps."

I left the stand, smiling to myself, impressed with this man.

A short time later I moved to Utah but I never forgot the story of this man and the boys—and their bartering.

Several years went by, each more rapid than the previous one. Just recently I had occasion to visit some old friends in that Idaho community and while I was there learned that Brother Miller had died.

They were having his viewing that evening and knowing my friends wanted to go, I agreed to accompany them.

Upon our arrival at the mortuary we fell into line to meet the relatives of the deceased and to offer whatever words of comfort we could. Ahead of us in line were three young men. One was in an Army uniform and the other two wore short haircuts, dark suits and white shirts—obviously potential bankers, lawyers, doctors, ministers, educators, or administrators.

They approached Sister Miller, standing, smiling and composed, by her husband's casket. Each of the young men hugged her, kissed her on the cheek, spoke briefly with her and moved on to the casket. Her misty light blue eyes followed them as, one by one, each young man stopped briefly and placed his own warm hand over the cold pale hand in the casket.

Each left the mortuary, awkwardly, wiping his eyes.

Our turn came to meet Sister Miller. I told her who I was and mentioned the story she had told me about the marbles. Eyes glistening she took my hand and led me to the casket.

"This is an amazing coincidence," she said. "Those three young men that just left were the boys I told you about. They just told me how they appreciated the things Jim 'traded' them. Now, at last, when Jim could not change his mind about color or size...they came to pay their debt.

"We've never had a great deal of the wealth of this world," she confided, "but, right now, Jim would consider himself the richest man in Idaho."

With loving gentleness she lifted the lifeless fingers of her deceased husband. Resting underneath were three magnificently shiny, red marbles.

A good name is more desirable than great riches,
to be esteemed is better than silver or gold.

PROVERBS 22:1

TOMMY

DAVID R. JOHNSON

FROM *THE LIGHT BEHIND THE STAR*

The bell over the shop door rang, and I looked up from my dish of frozen chocolate yogurt.

A stooped-over man entered and shuffled across the tile floor, his steps slow and measured. I guessed him to be in his late fifties to midsixties.

His baseball cap only partially hid a scalp covered with dry, flaky skin. His face was blotched red, not only from the heat, but also from a skin disorder. His stomach hung over his belt, and his pant legs were dragging the floor as he walked. His shirt tail hung free, and on his shirt pocket was pinned a paper name tag that said "Tommy." In his hand he clutched a metal lunch pail covered with stickers that advertised a local radio station. "Tommy" had all the outward signs of being mentally handicapped.

I wish I could say I spoke with him and asked how he was doing. But like the others in the shop, I tried to ignore the man. I went on eating my yogurt and talking with Frank, the other officer with me. We enjoyed the cool break we were able to get in two or three times a week during the hot summer.

From the corner of my eye I watched as Tommy dug into his pants pocket and laid the change on the counter for the store clerk to count. She asked what flavor of yogurt he wanted, then served him. Tommy sat down at one of the empty tables.

A small child at another table pointed at Tommy and asked, "What's wrong with that man, Mommy?" Others who came in saw Tommy sitting there, and then either bought their yogurt and left, or sat as far away from him as possible.

Frank and I finished eating and talked to a couple of children who wanted to "say hi to the nice policemen." I gave each of them one of the small plastic police badges I carry in my shirt pocket for just such an occasion.

As we started to leave, Tommy got up and walked over. He had yogurt around his smiling mouth. He stuck out his hand and said, "My name is Tommy."

I reached out and took his hand. The roughness of his diseased skin made me want to retrieve my hand as quickly as possible, but Tommy wouldn't let go. He just continued smiling and shaking. He said he liked policemen and wanted to be one.

I told him my name, and introduced him to Frank. Now Tommy released the grip on my hand and grabbed Frank's, and again held on and continued shaking. Finally we were able to get Tommy to release his grip, and we started out the door.

Tommy was right behind us. We turned around to him. Still smiling, he asked, "Can I have a badge too?"

I reached in my shirt pocket and pulled out the last one I had. Tommy's eyes lit up as he pinned it to his pocket. He thanked us, then walked back into the store to finish his yogurt.

Several days later, we made it back to the frozen yogurt shop and, sure enough, Tommy came in. He was excited to see us and called us by our names. I noticed he was wearing his plastic police badge right above his name.

He shuffled to the counter, and dug into his pocket. All he could pull out were some pieces of paper. I got up from the table, stepped to the counter, and asked Tommy what he wanted. "I'll buy it for you," I said.

He thanked me, then sat at his table and enjoyed his yogurt.

Over the next few months, Frank and I took turns buying Tommy his yogurt. We actually began looking forward to our times with him. He would sit at our table and tell us all about his day at the handicapped center where he worked.

Along with the ever present police badge, he occasionally wore a sign pinned to his shirt that told of some special award he had won: "First Place for Can Smashing," or, "First Place for Cleaning My Area." He was proud of his accomplishments, and excited to share them with us.

One day he wore a rather large colored sign that read "Today Is My Birthday." It was his sixty-second birthday—and we celebrated it with him.

One hot afternoon the dispatcher radioed a report to Frank of a possible drunk lying by the side of a store. I was close by, so I stopped to assist. When I got out of my car I saw a figure half lying and half sitting on the ground, with people walking quickly past him and pushing their children along to avoid any contact with him. I recognized the lunch pail—and then Tommy. He wasn't drunk, only overcome by the heat. His face was bathed in perspiration and his shirt was soaked through.

"Are you okay?" I asked, coming closer.

Tommy said only, "I fell down."

Frank and I helped him into the patrol car. Frank then drove him to his group home, where he found out Tommy had arthritis in both legs, which from time to time caused them to simply give out, making him fall.

Tommy recovered and was back on his feet in a few days.

The days turned into weeks, and the weeks into months. One day Frank and I realized we hadn't seen Tommy for some time. We decided to stop by his house and see how he was. While on our way there, I received a call for service, so Frank went on to Tommy's by himself.

Afterward Frank told me that he arrived just as a bus pulled to the curb in front of the group home. He watched as the bus driver helped Tommy get out. His arthritis had become worse, and now he could hardly walk without help.

Tommy was overjoyed to see Frank. He kept telling the other residents gathered around that Frank was his friend. Having a policeman for a friend made him an instant celebrity at the home.

We still visit Tommy from time to time, trying to spread a little sunshine in his life. (He especially likes it when we show up with a dish of frozen chocolate yogurt.) We've also found that Tommy puts quite a few rays of light into our lives too.

There are so many "Tommys" in the world today. We see them in our churches, at work, and in our neighborhoods—people who are mostly alone. I believe they're among the people with whom Jesus was identifying in Matthew 25—"I was hungry...I was thirsty...I was a stranger...I was naked...I was sick...I was in prison..."

You reach out to them in the same way Jesus said: "You gave me something to eat...you gave me drink...you invited me in...you clothed me...you visited me...you came to me..."

You can touch the lives of others with a simple act like taking a plate of cookies to the neighbor down the street, or inviting a fellow worker to lunch.

And if you're really pressed for ideas...take a dish of chocolate yogurt to Tommy. I know he'd like it—and you'd really like him.

ADVICE

BILLY GRAHAM

I heard about a young president of a company who instructed his secretary not to disturb him because he had an important appointment. The chairman of the board came in and said, "I want to see Mr. Jones." The secretary answered, "I'm terribly sorry, he cannot be disturbed; he has an important appointment."

The chairman became very angry. He banged open the door and saw the president of his corporation on his knees in prayer. The chairman softly closed the door and asked the secretary, "Is this usual?" And she said, "Yes, he does that every morning." To which the chairman of the board responded, "No wonder I come to him for advice."

THE ADMONITION SUIT

PHILIP GULLEY

FROM *HOME TOWN TALES*

One of the benefits of pastoring a small church is that you don't have to dress up. Most days I wear blue jeans, except on Sundays when I wear khakis and a sport coat. In the summer I wear short-sleeved shirts. A friend bought me a tie that has a picture of dogs playing poker on it. When I wear that, I have to sneak it out of the house and tie it on in the meetinghouse restroom. Otherwise, Joan won't let me out of the house.

I have one suit. It's charcoal gray with a suggestion of plaid. It looks like something you would wear to a funeral, which is the reason I bought it. That, and it was on sale for half price. I also wear it to weddings. On the rare occasion a fancy church invites me to speak, I wear it then, too. I have it cleaned once a year, which tells you how much I wear it.

One Sunday morning I was getting dressed for meeting. All my khakis were in the laundry basket. I had bought three identical pairs at the same time, on sale, and they were all dirty. Some of the men in our Quaker meeting wear blue jeans to church, but I didn't think I could get away with that. That left my suit, so I put it on, hid the dog tie in my pocket, and walked across the parking lot to the meetinghouse.

I stood at the meetinghouse door, greeting people. We have a number of vigorous hand-shakers and huggers in our meeting, so people would pump my hand, hug me, then comment on my suit. I explained that my khakis were dirty.

One of our members, Alice, is a dear ninety-one-year-old whose father had been a Quaker pastor. She liked that I was wearing a suit. Except for the dog tie, it reminded her of her father. "You look like a preacher today," she said. I think a great deal of Alice and was pleased to make her happy.

Harold is one of my best friends. He came up the walk, saw me in my suit, and said, "Uh-oh."

"What do you mean 'Uh-oh'?" I asked.

"You're wearing your admonition suit," Harold said. "Every time you wear a suit, we end up getting preached at."

That bothered me. It's a common perception that pastors are often angry about something. I can see why people think that. Once I watched a preacher on television with the sound turned off. It looked like he was yelling the whole time. So I try to project an image of a caring, gentle pastor. I even volunteer in the church nursery once a year. Now Harold was talking about my admonition suit.

The next month I wore my suit again. Harold grinned when he saw it but didn't say anything. When I rose to preach, I looked directly at him as I spoke. Harold fidgeted in his seat, waiting for the wrath of God to erupt. Instead, I talked about God's love. By the time I was finished speaking, Harold was exhausted. The anticipation of wrath had drained him of strength.

Despite his wisecracks about my suit, Harold is a soft touch, one of those rare souls who leave you feeling like royalty. When some people treat you that way, it's because they want you to buy something. Harold has nothing to sell.

Harold is the most forthright person I know. A lot of times we confuse gentleness with blandness. Harold is anything but bland. If he disagrees with you, he says so, but he does it so matter-of-factly it is disarming. You end up not minding one bit that Harold disagreed with you. When some people disagree with me, I try to change their minds. When Harold disagrees with me, I rethink my position.

Most of us borrow the opinions of others without much critical thought. Harold thinks a lot. I suspect that's what makes him gentle. True gentleness is grounded in knowledge. I think God is gentle because he knows us so well. It's easier to be gentle with people when you know their hurts.

When I first met Harold, he told me that he had grown up all over the world because his dad was in the military. Harold had been in the military too. I remember thinking that maybe God had brought us together so I could teach Harold what it meant to be a gentle, peace-loving Christian. That was four years ago. I've learned a lot since then.

I spend every Thursday evening with Harold and four other men. We sit around and read about the saints of old—Augustine and Luther and Calvin. I wonder if four hundred years from now folks will be studying Harold.

LOVE

HEART TO HEART

God did not create woman from man's head,

that he should command her,

nor from his feet,

that she should be his slave,

but rather from his side,

that she should be near his heart.

HEBREW PROVERB

BEN AND VIRGINIA

GWYN WILLIAMS

I n 1904, a railroad camp of civil engineers was set up near Knoxville, Tennessee. The L & N campsite had tents for the men, a warm campfire, a good cook and the most modern surveying equipment available. In fact, working as a young civil engineer for the railroad at the turn of the century presented only one real drawback: a severe shortage of eligible young women.

Benjamin Murrell was one such engineer. A tall, reticent man with a quiet sense of humor and a great sensitivity for people, Ben enjoyed the nomadic railroad life. His mother had died when he was only thirteen, and this early loss caused him to become a loner.

Like all the other men, Ben sometimes longed for the companionship of a young woman, but he kept his thoughts between himself and God. On one particularly memorable spring day, a marvelous piece of information was passed around the camp: The boss's sister-in-law was coming to visit! The men knew only three things about her: She was nineteen years old, she was single and she was pretty. By midafternoon the men could talk of little else. Her parents were sending her to escape the yellow fever that was invading the Deep South and she'd be there in only three days. Someone found a tintype of her, and the photograph was passed around with great seriousness and grunts of approval.

Ben watched the preoccupation of his friends with a smirk. He teased them for their silliness over a girl they'd never even met. "Just look at her, Ben. Take one look and then tell us you're not interested," one of the men retorted. But Ben only shook his head and walked away chuckling.

The next two days found it difficult for the men of the L & N engineering camp to concentrate. The train would be there early Saturday morning and they discussed their plan in great detail. Freshly bathed, twenty heads of hair carefully greased and slicked back, they would all be there to meet that train and give the young woman a railroad welcome she wouldn't soon forget. She'd scan the crowd, choose the most handsome of the lot and have an instant beau. Let the best man win, they decided. And each was determined to be that man.

The men were too preoccupied to see Ben's face as he beheld the picture of Virginia Grace for the first time. They didn't notice the way he cradled the photograph in his big hands like a lost treasure, or that he gazed at it for a long, long time. They missed the expression on his face as he looked first at the features of the delicate beauty, then at the camp full of men he suddenly perceived to be his rivals. And they didn't see Ben go into his tent, pick up a backpack and leave camp as the sun glowed red and sank beyond a distant mountain.

Early the next morning, the men of the L & N railroad camp gathered at the train station. Virginia's family, who had come to pick her up, rolled their eyes and tried unsuccessfully not to laugh. Faces were raw from unaccustomed shaves, and the combination of men's cheap colognes was almost obnoxious. Several of the men had even stopped to pick bouquets of wildflowers along the way.

At long last the whistle was heard and the eagerly awaited train pulled into the station. When the petite, vivacious little darling of the L & N camp stepped onto the platform, a collective sigh escaped her would-be suitors. She was even prettier than the tintype depicted. Then every man's heart sank in collective despair. For there, holding her arm in a proprietary manner and grinning from ear to ear, was Benjamin Murrell. And from the way she tilted her little head to smile up into his face, they knew their efforts were in vain.

"How," his friends demanded of Ben later, "did you do that?"

"Well," he said, "I knew I didn't have a chance with all you scoundrels around. I'd have to get to her first if I wanted her attention, so I walked down to the previous station and met the train. I introduced myself as a member of the welcoming committee from her new home."

"But the nearest station is seventeen miles away!" someone blurted incredulously. "You walked seventeen miles to meet her train? That would take all night?"

"That it did," he affirmed.

Benjamin Murrell courted Virginia Grace, and in due time they were married. They raised five children and buried one, a twelve-year-old son. I don't think they tried to build the eternal romance that some women's magazines claim is so important. Nor did they have a standing Friday night date. In fact, Ben was so far out in the sticks while working on one engineering job that one of their children was a full month old before he saw his new daughter. Ben didn't take Virginia to expensive restaurants, and the most romantic gift he ever brought her was an occasional jar of olives. If Virginia ever bought a fetching nightgown and chased him around the icebox, that secret remains buried with her to this day.

What I do know is that they worked together on their relationship by being faithful to one another, treating each other with consideration and respect, having a sense of humor, bringing up their children in the knowledge of love of the Lord, and loving one another through some very difficult circumstances.

I am one of Benjamin and Virginia's great-grandchildren. He died when I was a baby, unfortunately, so I have no memory of him. NaNa (Virginia) died when I was twelve and she was eighty-five. When I knew her she was a shriveled old woman who needed assistance to get around with a walker and whose back was hunched over from osteoporosis. Her aching joints were swollen with arthritis and her eyesight was hindered by the onset of glaucoma. At times, though, those clouded eyes would sparkle and dance with the vivaciousness of the girl my great-grandfather knew. They danced especially when she told her favorite story. It was the story of how she was so pretty that once, on the basis of a tintype, an entire camp turned out to meet the train and vie for her attention. It was the story of how one man walked seventeen miles, all night long, for a chance to meet the woman of his dreams and claim her for his wife.

IN A CATHEDRAL OF FENCE POSTS AND HARLEYS

NEIL PARKER

FROM *UNITED CHURCH OBSERVER*

I have had only two rules to guide which weddings I will do, and which I will turn down: I need to be able to meet with the bride and groom first, and I don't do weddings in unusual places—like parachuting or underwater.

But I broke both rules once, and it was the most meaningful wedding I ever celebrated.

I'd agreed to do this wedding on two days' notice when the minister who was to officiate was unavailable due to a family emergency. I had the details of the location (well out of town, on a farm); I knew the names of the bride and groom; and I knew that they'd done premarital sessions with the other minister.

I also knew something about their wedding guests and the particular setting they'd chosen for the celebration of their union. One hundred and forty bikers had come up to spend the weekend. And the wedding was to be an added bonus—and a surprise to all but a handful of the guests.

I confess to considerable misgivings as I turned off the highway onto the property and caught my first glimpse of the venue. Dozens of motorcycles filled the parking lot. Most were Harley-Davidsons, the choice of serious bikers. Very loud music filled the air from a tent and refreshment area in the center field. Tents dotted the landscape. It looked like a heavy-metal Woodstock.

Mine was the only Jetta in sight. I parked it and headed up to the house.

At least, to my relief, things seemed to be in order there. I was introduced to the bride's parents and the groom's parents while the bride was getting dressed. It didn't take long; jeans and a black T-shirt needed little more than a few flowers in the hair. The groom was introduced to me as Bear. It wasn't hard to know where the nickname came from; Bear outweighed me at least two to one. His beard was thick and bushy, and his arms were heavily tattooed. Bear didn't say much.

Once we'd checked to see that the license was in order and everything was ready, I headed down to the big tent. I don't push through crowds very well, meek and mild sort that I am, but I managed to get to the front, asked for a microphone, waited for the music to go silent, introduced myself, and announced that I was here for a wedding. I wasn't quite sure what reaction I was going to get.

Several of the bikers immediately headed to the parking lot. The air was filled with the throb of powerful engines revving. Then, with almost military precision, the bikes streamed out of the parking lot and straight towards the center field, heading directly towards me. A few feet away, they turned off to form a double row facing each other—an honor guard to create an aisle for the bride. With engines at full throttle, their roar echoed across the valley.

As the bride walked slowly and gracefully down this aisle, each bike she passed switched off its engine. As she passed the last pair, and all the engines were stilled, you could have heard a pin drop. She walked shyly up to Bear. His eyes were overflowing with tears. Then the birds started to sing.

All around the host couple were the congregation of their friends, members and families of the Sober Riders, each one a recovering alcoholic, each one a biker. Each one was bowed in prayer as we entered a holy moment.

The bride had given me only one instruction for the service: "Make sure you have a sermon," she said. "These people want to hear a word from God."

Her people. And, for an afternoon, my people. I stood in the middle of the field, in a congregation of T-shirts, jeans, and tattoos, in front of a groom and bride who knew exactly what they were doing and why, in a cathedral of fence posts and Harleys, and we gave thanks to God together.

MISTAKEN IDENTITY

Two ministers were discussing the advisability of writing down the names of brides and grooms to aid their memory at the ceremony. One minister said, "I once called the groom by the wrong name."

The other minister said, "I once started a ceremony and realized I couldn't remember whether the groom was John or James. I whispered to the groom, 'Is your name James or John?' 'James,' he replied. Then the bride nudged the groom and said, 'Your name is John.'"

EDWARD C. BOLAND

FROM *THE CHRISTIAN READER*

THE GOLD BOX

JAMES C. DOBSON

FROM *HOME WITH A HEART*

We sometimes learn the most from our children.

Some time ago, a friend of mine punished his three-year-old daughter for wasting a roll of gold wrapping paper. Money was tight, and he became infuriated when the child tried to decorate a box to put under the Christmas tree. Nevertheless, the little girl brought the gift to her father the next morning and said, "This is for you, Daddy." He was embarrassed by his earlier overreaction, but his anger flared again when he found that the box was empty.

He yelled at her, "Don't you know that when you give someone a present, there's supposed to be something inside of it?"

The little girl looked up at him with tears in her eyes and said, "Oh, Daddy, it's not empty. I blew kisses in the box. I filled it with my love. All for you, Daddy."

The father was crushed. He put his arms around his little girl, and he begged her for forgiveness. My friend told me that he kept that gold box by his bed for years. Whenever he was discouraged, he would take out an imaginary kiss and remember the love of the child who had put it there.

In a very real sense, each of us as parents has been given a gold container filled with unconditional love and kisses from our children. There is no more precious possession anyone could hold.

THE PORTRAIT

RON MEHL

FROM *THE TEN(DER) COMMANDMENTS*

I'm reminded of the story of a very wealthy man who, along with his son, shared a passion for collecting art. Together they traveled around the world, adding only the finest treasure to their collection. Priceless works by Picasso, Van Gogh, Monet, and many others adorned the walls of the family estate. The widowed elder man looked on with satisfaction as his only child became an experienced art collector in his own right. The son's trained eye and sharp business mind caused his father to beam with pride as they dealt with art dealers around the world.

As winter approached one year, war engulfed the nation, and the young man left to serve his country. After only a few short weeks, his father received a telegram. His beloved son was missing in action. The art collector awaited more news, fearing he would never see his son again. Within days, his worst fears were confirmed. The young man had died while attempting to evacuate a wounded fellow soldier.

Distraught and lonely, the old man faced the upcoming Christmas holidays with dread. What was left to celebrate? His joy was gone.

Early on Christmas morning, a knock on the door awakened the grieving man. As he walked to the door, the masterpieces of art on the walls seemed to mock him. Of what value were they without his son to share in their beauty? Opening the door, he was startled to see a young man in uniform. It was a soldier, with a large package in his hands. He introduced himself to the man.

"I was a friend to your son," he said. "As a matter of fact, I was the one he was rescuing when he died. May I come in for a few moments? I have something to show you."

As the two began to talk, the soldier told of how the man's son had talked so much about art, and the joy of collecting masterpieces alongside his father. "I'm something of an artist myself," the soldier said shyly. "And, well, I wanted you to have this."

As the old man unwrapped the package, the paper gave way to reveal a portrait of the man's son. Though the world would never consider it a work of genius, the painting somehow captured the young man's expression. The likeness was uncanny. Overcome with emotion, the man thanked the solider, promising to hang the picture above the fireplace.

A few hours later, after the soldier had departed, the old man set about his task. True to his word, the painting went above the fireplace, pushing aside a fortune in works of classic art. His task completed, the old man sat in his chair and spent Christmas day gazing at the gift he had been given.

During the days and weeks that followed, the man realized that even though his son was no longer with him, the boy's life would live on because of those he had touched. He would later learn that his son had rescued dozens of wounded soldiers before a bullet cut him down.

Fatherly pride and satisfaction began to ease the old man's grief. The painting of his son soon became his most prized possession, far eclipsing any interest in the pieces for which museums around the world clamored. He told his neighbors it was the greatest gift he had ever received.

The following spring, the old man became ill and passed away. With the famous collector's passing, the art world eagerly anticipated a great auction. According to the collector's will, all of the works would be auctioned on Christmas Day, the day he had received the greatest gift.

The day soon arrived and art dealers from around the world gathered to bid on some of the world's most spectacular paintings. Dreams would be fulfilled this day; many would soon claim, "I have the greatest collection." The auction began, however, with a painting that was not on any museum's list.

It was the simple portrait of a young soldier…the collector's son.

The auctioneer asked for an opening bid, but the room was silent. "Who will open with a bid of one hundred dollars?" he asked. Minutes passed and no one spoke. From the back of the room came a gruff voice, "Who cares about that painting? It's just a picture of his son." More voices echoed in agreement. "Let's forget about it and move on to the good stuff."

"No," the auctioneer replied. "We have to sell this one first. Now, who will take the son?"

Finally, a neighbor of the old man spoke. "Will you take ten dollars for the painting? That's all I can spare. I knew the boy, so I'd like to have it."

"I have ten dollars," called the auctioneer. "Will anyone go higher?" After more silence, the auctioneer said, "Going once, going twice, sold!" The gavel fell. Cheers filled the room and someone exclaimed, "Now we can get on with it."

But at that moment, the auctioneer looked up at the audience and quietly announced that the auction was over. Stunned disbelief blanketed the room. Finally someone spoke up. "What do you mean, it's over? We didn't come here for a picture of some old guy's son. What about all of these paintings? There are millions of dollars' worth of art here! I demand that you explain what is going on!"

The auctioneer replied, "It's very simple. According to the will of the father, whoever takes the son…gets it all."

FOR RICHER OR POORER

RETOLD BY ROCHELLE M. PENNINGTON

The wives who lived within the walls of the Weinsberg Castle in Germany were well aware of the riches it held: gold, silver, jewels, and wealth beyond belief.

Then the day came in 1141 A.D. when all their treasure was threatened. An enemy army had surrounded the castle and demanded the fortress, the fortune, and the lives of the men within. There was nothing to do but surrender.

Although the conquering commander had set a condition for the safe release of all women and children, the wives of Weinsberg refused to leave without having one of their own conditions met, as well. They demanded that they be allowed to fill their arms with as many possessions as they could carry out with them. Knowing that the women couldn't possibly make a dent in the massive fortune, their request was honored.

When the castle gates opened, the army outside was brought to tears. Each woman had carried out her husband.

The wives of Weinsberg, indeed, were well aware of the riches the castle held.

THE COLOR OF LOVE

ALLISON HARMS

My 98-year-old grandfather, always called Pa by our family, likes to give his gifts in a big way.

When I was about ten years old, Pa gave me one of the most memorable and definitely the largest personalized gift I've ever received. It taught me a lot about what love looks like.

My family went to visit Pa one July evening after supper. As the grown-ups admired his yard, us kids clambered up the granite boulder we had fondly dubbed "The George Washington Rock," our own mini Mt. Rushmore. When the grown-ups disappeared behind the arborvitae hedge, we followed. That's where Pa grew his vegetable garden. I remembered from other years how extraordinarily tidy he always kept it. Straight paths separated neat rows of well-trimmed plants and set off a border marked by marigolds. Every year, Pa carefully staked and tied his tomatoes and built intricate moats and mounds around his gourds, winter squash and melons. And even to a child who despised vegetables, his garden was pleasing to look at: its variety of textures and vivid greens, its symmetry altered only by sun and shadows.

When we caught up to the grown-ups by the garden, I gasped in surprise. This was not the model of vegetable geometry I had come to expect.

Instead, most of Pa's garden was covered with bicycle-tire-sized dusty leaves and vines thick as handlebars. Pigs' tail tendrils curled and stretched in every direction. Here and there star-shaped flowers bloomed, bright as orange California poppies. In a few places, where the flower had puckered into a fist, I could see a green, tennis-ball-sized fruit growing.

With his arms akimbo, Pa announced he had only put in a "postage stamp patch" of his usual garden produce this year because he was "going whole hog into pumpkins, *giant* pumpkins." He explained how he had started "Atlantic Giant" seeds indoors in paper cups ("only one seed per cup, mind you"). About two weeks later, he had transplanted the most vigorous seedling into some specially prepared, extra enriched soil in his garden. He gave the vine plenty of room to spread out—a square at least 25 feet per side—and mulched the soil with straw. He said he planned to put white sheets over the pumpkins when they grew above their leaf-shade canopy. I laughed, imagining squatty ghost-like bumps haunting the garden at noon instead of midnight. But Pa explained that without a covering, the skins of the ripening fruit would get sunburned. I slipped away as my mother and Pa started discussing what he should put under each of his prodigies to keep its undersides clean and free of rot and scarring. With the rest of the summer ahead of me and fifth grade in the fall, I soon forgot about Pa's pumpkins.

Until the middle of October, that is. Then Pa invited us for another visit. As soon as we tumbled out of the station wagon, he greeted us. Right away, I could tell something was up. Pa has never been the apple-cheeked, twinkly-eyed, merry-making kind of grandpa. He isn't demonstrative, except with his gifts, and always looked rather professorial with his wool vest and pipe. But that day he was different. It was as if he had a giggle bubbling in his chest that he had to keep swallowing so it wouldn't escape and embarrass him. He took us straight back to his garden.

Huge as harvest moons, there they were—two behemoth pumpkins. "Wow!" we said.

"Oh, my goodness sake!" my mother said.

Convinced we had been adequately awed from a distance, Pa took us in to get a closer look. My younger brother and I stepped tentatively over the prickly vines and through the scratchy leaves. We touched the smooth, cool skin of the pumpkins and tried to nudge them with the heels of our hands. We might as well have tried to move The George Washington Rock. Those bruisers would probably have sent the scale's arrow spinning to at least a quarter ton each.

But it was the silver scrawl across the top of one of the pumpkins that caught my attention. As the fruit grew, Pa had scratched my full name and birth date into its skin. The other pumpkin was inscribed with my younger brother's name and birth date. As a lower-middle child in a large family, I never assumed that anyone knew who I was or recognized me as an individual; I was just part of the passel, usually just the little sister of one of my older siblings. I often felt lost or left out, or simply overlooked. So when I discovered that Pa knew my whole name and exact birth date, when I realized he had grown that pumpkin thinking of just me, planning to surprise me at just the right time, I whooped for joy. I think I even dared to hug the old curmudgeon, or at least his legs. Later the thought of how much effort and time he had joyfully and secretly poured into that pumpkin touched me too.

Carved into the jack of all jack-o'-lanterns and then made into spice-scented pies and muffins, that pumpkin was definitely one of the most unusual gifts I've ever received. But more than that, it was just the right size to express Pa's giant generosity and fill a little girl's heart with the surprise of being loved.

Red may connote mere passion, but for me, orange is what real love looks like. For me, orange—bright, pumpkin orange—is the color of love. Definitely.

ROSES

DR. STEVE STEPHENS

Valentine's Day, and I tried my best to be a good husband. Like most men, I'm not always good at remembering the days that are significant to my wife, but I have learned over the years that, along with Mother's Day and our wedding anniversary, Valentine's Day is important.

This year, I knew I'd finally gotten it right: a gift beautifully wrapped with coordinated ribbons and bows, an emotionally charged card, a box of candy and six long-stemmed red roses. I walked casually into the kitchen, the roses in one hand behind my back. My wife and six-year-old daughter Brittany were sitting at the table.

"What day is it?" I asked, looking at my wife.

"Valentine's Day!" they said in unison.

I pulled the roses from behind my back as two sets of eyes lit up. So focused on my wife, I didn't see excitement turn to disappointment in my daughter's face when I filled only her mother's hands with treasures of my love. Hot tears filled little eyes and spilled down past a quivering chin to the table top.

In a single bound, I'd made my wife happy—and broken my little girl's heart. I gently scooped Brittany up with one arm as the other hand pulled a single rose from the bouquet. A shining smile returned. It was then that I learned that Valentine's Day is a time to give love—not only to my wife but to my children as well. Every member of the family needs to feel special and loved.

Now that we have three children, Valentine's Day comes each year with two hands full of roses: for Brittany, a delicate pink; for Dylan, yellow; and for Dusty, pure white. And my wife, who is special in a way like no other, still gets six long-stemmed red roses.

CLOSE CALL

My husband and I were driving toward our rural home when I spotted three deer about to cross in front of us. Noticing that my husband wasn't slowing down, I reached over, gently touched his arm, and said, "Honey...deer."

He still didn't slow down, so I repeated more firmly, "Honey...deer!"

Suddenly, he hit the brakes, veered, and managed to miss all three. After I caught my breath from our near-miss, I asked him why he hadn't paid attention when I warned him.

"Warned me?" he said. "I thought you were being romantic."

PATRICIA BEECHER

FROM *THE CHRISTIAN READER*

SIMPLE WOODEN BOXES

MARTHA PENDERGRASS TEMPLETON

FROM *ON LOVE*

I suppose everyone has a particular childhood Christmas that stands out more than any other. For me, it was the year that the Burlington factory in Scottsboro closed down. I was only a small child. I could not name for you the precise year; it is an insignificant blur in my mind, but the events of that Christmas will live forever in my heart.

My father, who had been employed at Burlington, never let on to us that we were having financial difficulties. After all, children live in a naive world in which money and jobs are nothing more than jabberwocky, and for us the excitement of Christmas could never be squelched. We knew only that our daddy, who usually worked long, difficult hours, was now home more than we had ever remembered; each day seemed to be a holiday.

Mama, a homemaker, now sought work in the local textile mills, but jobs were scarce. Time after time, she was told no openings were available before Christmas, and it was on the way home from one such distressing interview that she wrecked our only car. Daddy's meager unemployment check would now be our family's only source of income. For my parents, the Christmas season brought mounds of worries, crowds of sighs and tears and cascades of prayers.

I can only imagine what transpired between my parents in those moments when the answer came. Perhaps it took a while for the ideas to fully form. Perhaps it was a merging of ideas from both of my parents. I don't know for sure how the idea took life, but somehow it did. They would scrape together enough money to buy each of us a Barbie doll. For the rest of our presents, they would rely on their talents, using scraps of materials they already had.

While dark, calloused hands sawed, hammered and painted, nimble fingers fed dress after dress after dress into the sewing machine. Barbie-sized bridal gowns, evening gowns…miniature clothes for every imaginable occasion pushed forward from the rattling old machine. Where we were while all of this was taking place, I have no idea. But somehow my parents found time to pour themselves into our gifts, and the excitement of Christmas was once again born for the entire family.

That Christmas Eve, the sun was just setting over the distant horizon when I heard the roar of an unexpected motor in the driveway. Looking outside, I could hardly believe my eyes. Uncle Buck and Aunt Charlene, Mama's sister and her husband, had driven all the way from Georgia to surprise us. Packed tightly in their car, as though no air were needed, sat my three cousins, my "Aunt" Dean, who refused to be called "Aunt," and both my grandparents. I also couldn't help but notice innumerable gifts for all of us, all neatly packaged and tied with beautiful bows. They had known that it would be a difficult Christmas and they had come to help.

The next morning we awoke to more gifts than I ever could have imagined. And, though I don't have one specific memory of what any of the toys were, I know that there were mountains of toys. Toys! Toys! Toys!

And it was there, amidst all that jubilation, that Daddy decided not to give us his gifts. With all the toys we had gotten, there was no reason to give us the dollhouses that he had made. They were rustic and simple red boxes, after all. Certainly not as good as the store-bought gifts that Mama's family had brought. The music of laughter filled the morning, and we never suspected that, hidden somewhere, we each had another gift.

When Mama asked Daddy about the gifts, he confided his feelings, but she insisted he give us our gifts. And so, late that afternoon, after all of the guests had gone, Daddy reluctantly brought his gifts of love to the living room.

Wooden boxes. Wooden boxes, painted red, with hinged lids, so that each side could be opened and used as a house. On either side was a compartment just big enough to store a Barbie doll, and all the way across, a rack on which to hang our Barbie clothes. On the outside was a handle, so that when it was closed, held by a magnet that looked remarkably like an equal sign, the house could be carried suitcase style. And, though I don't really remember any of the other gifts I got that day, those boxes are indelibly etched into my mind. I remember the texture of the wood, the exact shade of red paint, the way the pull of the magnet felt when I closed the lid, the time-darkened handles and hinges…I remember how the clothes hung delicately on the hangers inside, and how I had to be careful not to pull Barbie's hair when I closed the lid. I remember everything that is possibly rememberable, because we kept and cherished those boxes long after our Barbie doll days were over.

I have lived and loved 29 Christmases, each new and fresh with an air of excitement all its own. Each filled with love and hope. Each bringing gifts, cherished and longed for. But few of those gifts compare with those simple wooden boxes. So it is no wonder that I get teary-eyed when I think of my father, standing there on that cold Christmas morning, wondering if his gift was good enough.

Love, Daddy, is always good enough.

POLITELY PARTISAN

LOIS WYSE

FROM *YOU WOULDN'T BELIEVE WHAT MY GRANDCHILD DID...*

They are old friends and new grandfathers, so when they met on the street, they embraced and began telling stories about their new babies.

"You wouldn't believe—" one grandfather began.

"—what my grandchild looks like," the other concluded.

"Want to see a picture?" they asked in unison.

And so each reached into his wallet and took out a picture, and together they stood and oohed and aahed.

It wasn't until the grandfathers had said their goodbyes and were seven blocks away from one another that each realized he had never looked at the picture of his friend's grandchild. Each had taken out the photo of his own grandchild and admired it; the happy grandpas had never bothered to exchange pictures.

ROMANCE

Bill Hybels

from *Fit to Be Tied*

R omance was never my strong suit. I proposed to Lynne in her parents' garage; I took my Harley-Davidson on our honeymoon; I thought our best anniversary was the one we spent watching a video of *Rocky III*. I had to grow in the gentle art of romance.

So, for starters, I figured that meant flowers. Beyond that, I didn't have a clue, but I knew I could get the flower job done. As confirmation from God that I was moving in the right direction, who do you think set up shop right out of the trunk of his '58 DeSoto at the corner opposite our church? The flower man!

So, quite regularly, on my way home from work or from meetings, I would pull over to the side of the road, buy a bundle of roses or carnations from the flower man, and take them home to Lynne. *What a husband!* I thought as I handed over my three bucks.

Yet when I proudly presented these flowers to Lynne, fully expecting her to hire the Marine Corps Band to play "Hail to the Chief," her response was rather lukewarm.

"Gee, thanks," she said. "Where'd you get these?"

"Where else? My buddy, the flower man—you know, the guy with the '58 DeSoto at Barrington and Algonquin. I'm a volume buyer now.

Because I stop there so often he gives me a buck off, and if they're a little wilted, he gives me two bucks off. I figure they'll perk up when you put them in water."

"Of course," she said.

I did that regularly for quite some time—until Lynne's lack of enthusiasm for the gift drained my enthusiasm for the practice.

Some time later, at our regularly scheduled date night, Lynne and I decided to clear the air on anything that might be bothering either of us. We do that now and then. We sit down in a cheap restaurant (not only am I unromantic, I'm also Dutch) and say, "What's going on? Is there anything we need to talk about? Is there anything amiss in our relationship?" On that particular night, Lynne took out her list and started checking off the items, and I said, "Ooooh, you're right on that one. Sorry. Eeeh, that one too. Yep. Guilty as charged. Guilty. Guilty. You're right again." She ended her list, and I was in a pile. I said, "I really am sorry, but trust me. I'm going to do better."

She said, "Now, what about you?" I really didn't have any complaints, but after hearing her grocery list, I thought I should say *something*. I scrambled. "Well, I do have one little problem. Have you noticed the absence of the flowers lately?"

"No," she said. "I haven't really paid attention." *How could she say that?*

"We have a problem. I can't figure it out. Hundreds of thousands of husbands pass by that corner. Do they stop for flowers? No. Do I stop? Yes!…What gives? What is your problem?"

Her answer made my head spin. She looked me straight in the eyes and quietly said, "The truth is, Bill, I'm not impressed when you give me half-dead flowers that come out of the trunk of a '58 DeSoto that you were lucky enough to run into on your way home from work. The flowers are cheap and the effort is minimal. The way I see it, you're not investing enough time or energy to warrant a wholehearted response from me. You're not thinking about what would make me happy; you're just doing what's convenient for you."

I said, "Okay, let's get this straight. You would be happier if I got up from my desk in the middle of my busy day, threw my study schedule to the wind, walked all the way across the parking lot, got in my car, made a special trip to Barrington where I'd have to pay quadruple the price just because it said Barrington on the bag? And you wouldn't mind if the extra time that took would crimp my work schedule at the Y.... And you wouldn't mind if I came home late because of *all* the extra running around I would have to do to get you *expensive* flowers? Is *that* what you're telling me? *That* would make you happy?"

Without batting an eyelash, Lynne said, "Yes, that would make me happy."

I couldn't believe it! "What're you talking about? What you're asking for is neither practical, economical, nor an efficient use of time."

"That's a great definition of romance, Bill. You're learning!"

May you rejoice in the wife of your youth;
May you ever be captivated by her love.

PROVERBS 5:18–19

IN THE TRENCHES

STU WEBER

FROM *LOCKING ARMS*

You've probably heard the powerful story coming out of World War I of the deep friendship of two soldiers in the trenches. Two buddies were serving together in the mud and misery of that wretched European stalemate (one version even identifies them as actual brothers). Month after month they lived out their lives in the trenches, in the cold and the mud, under fire and under orders.

From time to time one side or the other would rise up out of the trenches, fling their bodies against the opposing line and slink back to lick their wounds, bury their dead, and wait to do it all over again. In the process, friendships were forged in the misery. Two soldiers became particularly close. Day after day, night after night, terror after terror, they talked of life, of families, of hopes, of what they would do when (and if) they returned from this horror.

On one more fruitless charge, "Jim" fell, severely wounded. His friend, "Bill," made it back to the relative safety of the trenches. Meanwhile Jim lay suffering beneath the night flares. Between the trenches. Alone.

The shelling continued. The danger was at its peak. Between the trenches was no place to be. Still, Bill wished to reach his friend, to comfort him, to offer what encouragement only friends can offer. The officer in charge refused to let Bill leave the trench. It was simply too dangerous. As he turned his back, however, Bill went over the top. Ignoring the smell of cordite in the air, the concussion of incoming rounds, and the pounding in his chest, Bill made it to Jim.

Sometime later he managed to get Jim back to the safety of the trenches. Too late. His friend was gone. The somewhat self-righteous officer, seeing Jim's body, cynically asked Bill if it had been "worth the risk." Bill's response was without hesitation.

"Yes, sir, it was," he said. "My friend's last words made it more than worth it. He looked up at me and said, 'I knew you'd come.'"

We too often love things and use people,
when we should be using things and loving people.

AUTHOR UNKNOWN

A MILLION, MILLION

DEBI STACK

Daddy, how much did I cost?"

Perched on my parents' bedroom cedar chest, I listened to their casual talk about budgets and paychecks—talk as relevant back in 1967 as it is today. My then six-year-old mind concluded, wrongly, that my family was poor.

Dad stood at his dresser, looking at bills. He wore faded jeans, an undershirt, and white canvas shoes stained grass-green from mowing our lawn. Mom folded laundry on the bed, making even towers of sun-dried clothes. I spotted my new shorts sets and thought about day camp.

Their money talk continued, and Dad joined me on the cedar chest. I plucked the springy metal watchband on Dad's tan wrist, thinking that the white skin underneath reminded me of a fish belly. Just as I started to ask him to "make a muscle" so I could try pushing his flexed biceps down, a thought hit me like icy water from a garden hose: *Dad had to pay for me.*

While the story of my birth ranked as a bedtime favorite, I had never considered hospital bills...or the countless meals I'd eaten...or the price of summer clothes.

"Daddy," I interrupted again, "how much did I cost?"

"Oh, let's see." He sighed in distraction and placed his watch on the safety of his dresser. "About a million dollars."

A light went out inside of me. *A million dollars.* Because of me, Dad worked two jobs. Because of me, he drove an old car, ate lunch at home, and had his dress shoes resoled—again.

With my eyes and chin down, I inched off the cedar chest and shuffled into the kitchen. From a shelf, I took my granny-shaped bank which held every penny I owned—seven dollars even. And not seven dollars in assorted change, but seven cool, shiny silver dollars. One for every birthday, and one for the day I was born.

The bank's rubber plug surrendered, and the coins poured into my damp hands. I had often played with these coins in secret, jostling them in a small drawstring bag in my roles as gypsy or runaway princess. They had always been put back in the bank, though, and I felt secure pleasure in just knowing they were there. But that day, the "clink" of returning each coin sounded hollow.

If the topic had changed when I returned to my parents' bedroom, I didn't notice. Tugging on Dad's shirt, I held out my first payment on a million dollars.

"Here," I sniffed. "Maybe this will help pay for me."

"What?" Dad's confused look matched my own. Didn't he remember what he'd said? Didn't the sight of me remind him of how much I cost?

My tear-filled eyes, which I couldn't seem to take away from the bank, finally made sense to him.

Dad knelt down and pulled me close. "You didn't cost a million dollars, but you're worth a *million*-million dollars. And if that's what I'd have to pay for you, I'd do it. Now dry those eyes and put your bank away."

At the time, I felt some relief that Dad didn't have a million-dollar debt, but more relief that I hadn't lost my silver dollars.

Today, I often pull this memory out, turn it over, and feel the warm, satisfied weight of it in my heart. Back then, no price could be put on my worth to my dad. No price can be put on his worth to me now.

Thanks, Dad. I love you, too.

TWENTY WAYS TO MAKE YOUR WIFE FEEL SPECIAL

AL GRAY

FROM *LISTS TO LIVE BY*

1. Ask her to dance when you hear your love song.
2. Polish her shoes for special occasions.
3. Have good conversation when you'd rather read the paper.
4. Give her a back rub with no expectations of making love.
5. Buy and plant a rose bush as a surprise.
6. Keep your home repaired and in good order.
7. Make sure the car has good tires and is in good running condition.
8. Hold her hand when you lead the family in prayer.
9. Write out a list of all your important documents and where you keep them.
10. Find a way to save something from every paycheck.
11. Ask her input before making decisions.
12. Hold her tenderly when she cries and tell her it's okay.
13. Ask her out and plan the complete date yourself, including making reservations.
14. Occasionally, eat quiche and dainty desserts at a Victorian restaurant.
15. Understand when she forgets to enter a check in the ledger.
16. Shave on your day off.
17. Call if you're going to be more than fifteen minutes late.
18. Encourage her to take time with her friends.
19. Remember to carry a clean handkerchief when you go to a romantic movie.
20. Tell her she will always be beautiful when she worries about getting older.

THE EYES OF THE HEART

Luci Swindoll

from *We Brake for Joy!*

The filthy station wagon pulled into the car wash, loaded with kids and a driver who looked as if he hadn't shaved in weeks. With his hair tousled and a cigarette hanging out of the right side of his mouth, he was wearing clothes he probably had slept in. When he stopped, all eyes turned toward him.

Hairy Dicer, if I ever saw one, I thought to myself. A friend of mine called anybody "Hairy Dicer" who had those little fur dice hanging from his rearview mirror. This guy took the prize.

He opened the back of the station wagon and began to lift out the occupants. One by one he hugged and kissed each child, whom he gently lowered to the ground. Then they romped and played with one another and their father to their little hearts' content. I knew they were his children because over and over they called him "Daddy."

"Oh, Daddy, play with us. Daddy, throw me the ball. Look, Daddy, look at this. I can do that, Daddy...watch!"

Slowly, lovingly, deliberately, this disheveled man gave attention to all six children, playing, talking, laughing, discovering...and together they had a wonderful time. I sat, astonished and ashamed of myself for thinking the guy was a creep....

Who cares if the guy at the car wash was the opposite of my view of a proper dad? All those kids cared about was the attention he gave them. He listened. He played. He loved them.

And, you know what is really amazing? When I saw his heart...with my heart...he became almost good-looking. Well, maybe not good-looking, but certainly more appealing. I saw him with different eyes, the eyes of nonjudgment. I liked him.

THE ONE THE FATHER
LOVES THE MOST

BRENNAN MANNING

FROM *LION AND LAMB*

A professor of mine once told me the following story: "I'm one of thirteen children. One day when I was playing in the street of our hometown, I got thirsty and came into the house for a glass of water. My father had just come home from work to have lunch. He was sitting at the kitchen table with a neighbor. A door separated the kitchen from the pantry and my father didn't know I was there. The neighbor said to my father, 'Joe, there's something I've wanted to ask you for a long time. You have thirteen children. Out of all of them is there one that is your favorite, one you love more than all the others?'"

"I had my ear pressed against the door hoping against hope it would be me. 'That's easy,' my father said. 'That's Mary, the twelve-year-old. She just got braces on her teeth and feels so awkward and embarrassed that she won't go out of the house anymore. Oh, but you asked about my favorite. That's my twenty-three-year-old, Peter. His fiancée just broke their engagement, and he is desolate. But the one I really love the most is little Michael. He's totally uncoordinated and terrible in any sport he tries to play. But, of course, the apple of my eye is Susan. Only twenty-four, living in her own apartment, and developing a drinking problem. I cry for Susan. But I guess of all the kids...' and my father went on mentioning each of his thirteen children by name."

The professor ended his story saying: "What I learned was that the one my father loved most was the one who needed him most at that time. And that's the way the Father of Jesus is: he loves those most who need him most, who rely on him, depend upon him, and trust him in everything. Little he cares whether you've been as pure as St. John or as sinful as Mary Magdalene. All that matters is trust. It seems to me that learning how to trust God defines the meaning of Christian living. God doesn't wait until we have our moral life in order before he starts loving us."

MOTIVATION

PERSISTENCE

We cannot go back and make a new start,
But we can start now to make a new ending.

FRANKLIN COVEY

FROM *SUCCESSORIES, INC.*

FLOWERS AND WEEDS

PHILIP GULLEY

FROM *HOME TOWN TALES*

Once a year my wife has a birthday. It's been that way as long as I've known her. Every year it's the same problem—what do you get the woman who has everything? Most of the time I buy her jewelry. One time I gave her a bracelet. She told me it was so beautiful she'd hate to lose it. So she put it in her jewelry box, where it's been ever since. It's still in perfect condition. She's taken fine care of it.

I decided one year to give her something she could use. Our iron was making funny noises on the steam setting, so I thought I would buy her a new iron. I asked my sister her opinion. She told me not to buy Joan an iron, that it wasn't very romantic. I'm glad I listened to my sister. Irons aren't very romantic. It would be like giving someone a vacuum cleaner. The boys and I went to Furrow's Hardware and bought her a wheelbarrow instead.

The week before, Joan and the boys had been outside cleaning up the yard, picking up sticks and putting them in the wheelbarrow. The load was unbalanced, and the wheelbarrow kept tipping over whenever Joan pushed it. So I bought her a wheelbarrow with two wheels. I don't mean to boast, but that kind of thoughtful consideration has enabled our marriage to flourish.

Whenever Joan works in the yard, she takes the boys with her. She's teaching them the difference between weeds and flowers. They're not in school yet, but they can already distinguish between wild bloodwort and shepherd's purse. Joan wants them to know these things before they're turned loose to hoe the flower beds. Though it isn't an easy lesson to teach, it's an important one to learn. Otherwise, they'll spend their lives confusing weeds for flowers and flowers for weeds.

Buying my wife a new wheelbarrow raised the problem of what to do with the old one. The tire had a slow leak. Every time we used it, we had to pump up the tire. If we used it more than an hour, we had to put more air in it. It's been like that all ten years we've owned it, a burden from day one. I filled the tire, hosed off the wheelbarrow, hung a *Free* sign on it, and hauled it to the curb.

A man down the street spied it, shiny and red, glistening in the sun, tire full. He wheeled it across the street to his yard, delighted with his unexpected find. I drove by his house later that day. He was pushing the wheelbarrow across his yard. It was full of sticks; the tire was flat. It tipped over and the sticks fell out. He began kicking the wheelbarrow. I could hear him cuss and swear. Ordinarily, he is a saintly man, but that wheelbarrow has tarnished many a halo.

This man has been living under a burden since the day he took up with that wheelbarrow. One falling domino after another. Because he didn't pick up the sticks, he rolled over a limb and broke his mower. While he was shopping for a new one, the dandelions moved in and took over. He ended up having to spray his entire yard. I was going to offer my help, but by then he wasn't speaking to me. All of this from a wheelbarrow marked *Free.*

We take some things into our lives which have a veneer of blessing, and they exact a price we can scarcely imagine. We confuse bane for blessing and blessing for bane. I watch Joan teach our sons the difference between flower and weed. I hope it will be a primer for their later years, that those garden lessons will be their start in lives of wise discernment. I hope they'll learn that just because something's sitting at the curb marked *Free,* doesn't mean it really is.

Jesus once taught about how the cares of the world can grind a plant down to nothing. These "cares" are the things we bring into our lives with scarcely a thought. They promise good and deliver ill—the material goods that enslave us, the relationships that crush our spirits, the careers that tax our souls. Most all of us have a flat-tired wheelbarrow haunting us one way or another. It helps to learn the difference between weeds and flowers, whether something should be left sitting at the curb or carried home with joy.

SUCCESS

Someday I hope to enjoy enough of what the world calls success
so that someone will ask me, "What's the secret of it?"
I shall say simply this: "I get up when I fall down."

PAUL HARVEY

THE GOOD LIFE

ALAN LOY MCGINNIS

FROM *THE BALANCED LIFE*

I once knew a man, born illegitimate in Pennsylvania in the 1890s, at a time when our society heaped terrible opprobrium on such children as they grew up. He once told me that he and his mother lived in a small town where it was common knowledge who his father was, but that he did not ever recall having a conversation with the man. As one might expect, he dropped out of school to work, became a hard drinker and something of a barroom brawler. But then he fell in love with a gentle, beautiful young farm girl. They married and soon thereafter became born-again Christians. "I guess a strong simple faith was what a guy like me needed," he once told me, and for the next fifty years he lived that faith powerfully. Moving to Indiana in the Depression, he eventually found a job in a steel mill and spent the rest of his life working there among hard-working, hard-drinking, hard-living men. Though they teased him about being different, they came to respect him for the fact that he never swore, the way he talked quietly about how much his faith meant to him, and the depth of his generosity that caused him to lend them money or help them in many other ways when they were in trouble. Eventually he worked his way up to lead man, then finally became a foreman in the plant. The family had four children, and he and his wife provided a stable environment where there was strong discipline, but where the children also knew unquestionably that they were loved. As one might expect, that love has been transferred to his children's children and their progeny. All four of his children have distinguished themselves. (They are lawyers, engineers, teachers, and one son became superintendent of the steel mill where my friend had worked—fortunately when he was still alive to enjoy his son's accomplishments.)

Through an unusual set of circumstances, I had occasion to observe that man and his family very closely over the course of twenty years, and he became like a father to me. During that time we had some long, quiet talks. He talked to me once about the fact that when he was promoted to foreman at the plant, he found he was in over his head. He simply had not had enough math in school to do the intricate calculations necessary or enough English to write the reports required. "I knew a lot about steel," he told me, smiling, "but I never was a good speller. So, I went to the superintendent one day and told him I'd like my old job back. I said I appreciated the confidence they'd placed in me, and that I'd given it my best, but didn't think I could do the job as adequately as they deserved. He looked at me like I was crazy, because he knew I needed the money, but when I went back to working on the line I was a lot happier. I was where I belonged."

When my friend told me that story, I watched him closely to see if there was a twinge of regret in his eyes. There was not. Here was a man who had not had nearly the educational opportunities he deserved and had grown up embarrassed about other things over which he had no control, but any bitterness about those years had long since been washed away by his faith. He had raised four children in his small, neatly kept house, sent them all to college, and by the time he told me that story, he was basking in the delight of coming to the end of a life into which much love had been packed. A granddaughter told me that one of the things she admired was that he seemed to have no fear of dying: "One day he told me he'd had a good life and was having a lot of fun in retirement, but that he was ready to go to heaven anytime the Lord decided to take him."

I was unable to be at that couple's fiftieth wedding anniversary celebration, but I understand it was a large gathering, with dozens of children, grandchildren, great-grandchildren, and many friends. Was that man a success? An unqualified one. When such faith, integrity, and generosity have been combined in a person's days, the result is a balanced life. Or what Tolstoy called a "magnificent life"—working for the people one loves and loving one's work.

Opportunity is missed by most people because it is
dressed in overalls and looks like work.

THOMAS A. EDISON

I WANT THAT ONE

CHARLES STANLEY

FROM *HOW TO KEEP YOUR KIDS ON YOUR TEAM*

I heard a story once about a farmer who had some puppies for sale. He made a sign advertising the pups and nailed it to a post on the edge of his yard. As he was nailing the sign to the post, he felt a tug on his overalls. He looked down to see a little boy with a big grin and something in his hand.

"Mister," he said, "I want to buy one of your puppies."

"Well," said the farmer, "these puppies come from fine parents and cost a good deal."

The boy dropped his head for a moment, then looked back up at the farmer and said, "I've got thirty-nine cents. Is that enough to take a look?"

"Sure," said the farmer, and with that he whistled and called out, "Dolly. Here, Dolly." Out from the doghouse and down the ramp ran Dolly followed by four little balls of fur. The little boy's eyes danced with delight.

Then out from the doghouse peeked another little ball; this one noticeably smaller. Down the ramp it slid and began hobbling in an unrewarded attempt to catch up with the others. The pup was clearly the runt of the litter.

The little boy pressed his face to the fence and cried out, "I want that one," pointing to the runt.

The farmer knelt down and said, "Son, you don't want that puppy. He will never be able to run and play with you the way you would like."

With that the boy reached down and slowly pulled up one leg of his trousers. In doing so he revealed a steel brace running down both sides of his leg attaching itself to a specially made shoe. Looking up at the farmer, he said, "You see, sir, I don't run too well myself, and he will need someone who understands."

You can get everything in life you want, if
you will just help enough other people get what they want.

ZIG ZIGLAR

A GIFT FROM THE SCRAP PILE

BARBARA JOHNSON

FROM *WE BRAKE FOR JOY!*

harles Darrow was out of work and as poor as a pauper during the Depression, but he kept a smile on his face and a sparkle in his eye. He didn't want his wife, expecting their first child, to be discouraged; so every night when he returned to their little apartment after standing in the unemployment lines all day, he would tell her funny stories about the things he had seen—or imagined.

Darrow was a clever man, and he was always coming up with notions that made people laugh. (He wasn't at all like the lady who said she once had a bright idea—but it died of loneliness.)

Darrow knew how powerfully his own attitude affected his wife. His temperament was the color his wife used to paint her own mood. If he came home weary and irritable, her spirits fell, and her smile vanished. On the other hand, if she heard him whistling a merry tune as he climbed the many flights of stairs up to their tiny rooms, she would fling open the door and scamper out to the railing to lean over and smile at him as he wound his way up the staircase. They fed on the gift of each other's joy.

In his younger years, Darrow had enjoyed happy family vacations in nearby Atlantic City, and he drew on those memories to keep his spirits high. He developed a little game on a square piece of cardboard. Around the edges he drew a series of "properties" named after the streets and familiar places he had visited during those pleasant childhood summers. He carved little houses and hotels out of scraps of wood, and as he and his young wife played the game each evening, they pretended to be rich, buying and selling property and "building" homes and hotels like extravagant tycoons. On those long, dark evenings, that impoverished apartment was filled with the sound of laughter.

Charles Darrow didn't set out to become a millionaire when he developed "Monopoly," the game that was later marketed around the world by Parker Brothers, but that's what happened. The little gift he developed from scraps of cardboard and tiny pieces of wood was simply a way to keep his wife's spirits up during her Depression-era pregnancy; ultimately, that gift came back to him as bountiful riches.

Monopoly is still being sold by the thousands more than fifty years later. Every time I think of those little green houses and red hotels, the unusual game pieces, and those "get out of jail" cards that made us all race around the game board with gleeful abandon, I see an example of shared joy. Darrow created a gift of joy, shared it with the world, and the gift came right back to him a thousand-fold.

The greatest thing in the world is not so much where we stand as in what direction we're moving.

OLIVER WENDELL HOLMES

A MAN CAN'T JUST SIT AROUND

HOWARD HENDRICKS WITH CHIP MACGREGOR

FROM *STANDING TOGETHER*

I suppose most people have dreams, but how many people actually turn their dreams into reality? Larry Walters is among the relatively few who have. His story is true, though you may find it hard to believe.

Larry was a truck driver, but his lifelong dream was to fly. When he graduated from high school, he joined the Air Force in hopes of becoming a pilot. Unfortunately, poor eyesight disqualified him. So when he finally left the service, he had to satisfy himself with watching others fly the fighter jets that crisscrossed the skies over his backyard. As he sat there in his lawn chair, he dreamed about the magic of flying.

Then one day, Larry Walters got an idea. He went down to the local army-navy surplus store and bought a tank of helium and forty-five weather balloons. These were not your brightly colored party balloons, these were heavy-duty spheres measuring more than four feet across when fully inflated.

Back in his yard, Larry used straps to attach the balloons to his lawn chair, the kind you might have in your own backyard. He anchored the chair to the bumper of his jeep and inflated the balloons with helium. Then he packed some sandwiches and drinks and loaded a BB gun, figuring he could pop a few of those balloons when it was time to return to earth.

His preparations complete, Larry Walters sat in his chair and cut the anchoring cord. His plan was to lazily float back down to terra firma. But things didn't quite work out that way.

When Larry cut the cord, he didn't float lazily up; he shot up as if fired from a cannon! Nor did he go up a couple hundred feet. He climbed and climbed until he finally leveled off at eleven thousand feet! At that height, he could hardly risk deflating any of the balloons, lest he unbalance the load and really experience flying! So he stayed up there, sailing around for fourteen hours, totally at a loss as to how to get down.

Eventually, Larry drifted into the approach corridor for Los Angeles International Airport. A Pan Am pilot radioed the tower about passing a guy in a lawn chair at eleven thousand feet with a gun in his lap. (Now there's a conversation I'd have given anything to have heard!)

LAX is right on the ocean, and you may know that at nightfall, the winds on the coast begin to change. So, as dusk fell, Larry began drifting out to sea. At that point, the Navy dispatched a helicopter to rescue him. But the rescue team had a hard time getting to him, because the draft from their propeller kept pushing his home-made contraption farther and farther away. Eventually they were able to hover over him and drop a rescue line with which they gradually hauled him back to earth.

As soon as Larry hit the ground he was arrested. But as he was being led away in handcuffs, a television reporter called out, "Mr. Walters, why'd you do it?" Larry stopped, eyed the man, then replied nonchalantly, "A man can't just sit around."

RUNNING AFTER SUCCESS

RABBI HAROLD S. KUSHNER

FROM *WHEN ALL YOU'VE EVER WANTED ISN'T ENOUGH*

A rabbi once approached a member of his congregation and said, "Whenever I see you, you're always in a hurry. Tell me, where are you running all the time?" The man answered, "I'm running after success, I'm running after fulfillment, I'm running after the reward for all my hard work." The rabbi responded, "That's a good answer if you assume that all those blessings are somewhere ahead of you, trying to elude you, and if you run fast enough, you may catch up with them. But isn't it possible that those blessings are behind you, that they are looking for you, and the more you run, the harder you make it for them to find you?"

HEAD HUNTER

JOSH MCDOWELL

FROM *BUILDING YOUR SELF IMAGE*

An executive hirer, a "head-hunter" who goes out and hires corporation executives for other firms, once told me, "When I get an executive that I'm trying to hire for someone else, I like to disarm him. I offer him a drink, take my coat off, then my vest, undo my tie, throw up my feet and talk about baseball, football, family, whatever, until he's all relaxed. Then, when I think I've got him relaxed, I lean over, look him square in the eye and say, 'What's your purpose in life?' It's amazing how top executives fall apart at that question.

"Well, I was interviewing this fellow the other day, had him all disarmed, with my feet up on his desk, talking about football. Then I leaned up and said, 'What's your purpose in life, Bob?' And he said, without blinking an eye, 'To go to heaven and take as many people with me as I can.' For the first time in my career I was speechless."

THE TROUBLE TREE

AUTHOR UNKNOWN

The carpenter I hired to help me restore an old farmhouse had just finished a rough first day on the job. A flat tire made him lose an hour of work, his electric saw quit, and now his ancient pickup truck refused to start.

While I drove him home, he sat in stony silence. On arriving, he invited me in to meet his family. As we walked toward the front door, he paused briefly at a small tree, touching tips of the branches with both hands. When opening the door, he underwent an amazing transformation. His tanned face was wreathed in smiles and he hugged his two small children and gave his wife a kiss.

Afterward he walked me to the car. We passed the tree and my curiosity got the better of me. I asked him about what I had seen him do earlier. "Oh, that's my trouble tree," he replied. "I know I can't help having troubles on the job, but one thing's for sure. Troubles don't belong in the house with my wife and the children. So I just hang them up on the tree every night when I come home. Then in the morning I pick them up again."

"Funny thing is," he smiled, "when I come out in the morning to pick 'em up, there ain't nearly as many as I remember hanging up the night before."

SKILLFUL HANDS

EUGENE H. PETERSON

FROM *RUN WITH THE HORSES*

I once knew a man who had come to this country after World War II as a displaced person. He had been a skilled cabinetmaker in his home country but after the war had to settle for a job as sexton in a church. Not long after I became a pastor in that same church, I also became a father. Toys began to accumulate around the house. Knowing of his dexterity with tools and lumber, I asked Gus if he would throw together a toy box for me when he had a few minutes. I wanted a storage bin for the boys; I knew Gus could do it in an hour or so.

Weeks later he presented our family with a carefully designed and skillfully crafted toy box. My casual request had not been treated casually. I was pleased, but also embarrassed. I was embarrassed because what I thought would be done in an hour had taken many hours of work. I expressed my embarrassment. I laced my gratitude with apologies. His wife reproached me, "But you must understand that Gus is a cabinet-maker. He could never, as you say, 'throw' a box together. His pride would not permit it."

That toy box has been in our family for over twenty years now and rebukes me whenever I am tempted to do hasty or shoddy work of any kind.

ALL IT TAKES IS
A LITTLE MOTIVATION

ZIG ZIGLAR

FROM *OVER THE TOP*

I love the story the late Dr. Ken McFarland delighted in telling.
It seems a gentleman worked on the 4:00 P.M. to midnight shift, and he always walked home after work. One night the moon was shining so bright he decided to take a shortcut through the cemetery, which would save him roughly a half-mile walk. There were no incidents involved, so he repeated the process on a regular basis, always following the same path. One night as he was walking his route through the cemetery, he did not realize that during the day a grave had been dug in the very center of his path. He stepped right into the grave and immediately started desperately trying to get out. His best efforts failed him, and after a few minutes, he decided to relax and wait until morning when someone would help him out.

He sat down in the corner and was half asleep when a drunk stumbled into the grave. His arrival roused the shift worker since the drunk was desperately trying to climb out, clawing frantically at the sides. Our hero reached out his hand, touched the drunk on the leg, and said, "Friend, you can't get out of here…"—but he did! Now that's motivation!

LESSON FROM
THE PRAIRIE

AUTHOR UNKNOWN

There's an old story out of the American West about how cattle act in winter storms.

Sometimes the storms took a heavy toll. They would start with freezing rains. Temperatures would plummet below zero. Then, bitterly cold winds would begin to pile up huge snowdrifts. Most cattle turned their backs to the icy blasts and they would begin to move downwind until they came up against the inevitable barbed wire fence. In the big storms, they would pile up against the fence and die by the score.

But one breed always survived. Herefords would instinctively head into the wind. They would stand shoulder to shoulder, heads down, facing the blasts.

As one cowboy once put it, "You most always found the Herefords alive and well. I guess that's the greatest lesson I ever learned on the prairies—just face life's storms."

TWO DIARIES

STEVEN J. LAWSON

FROM *THE LEGACY*

At the constant request of his young son, a busy dad took a day off to go fishing. It was just the two of them. Leaving behind a desk cluttered with unfinished business, the father drove to a secluded lake where they spent the day together fishing, rowing, talking, and fishing some more.

Throughout the day, all the father could think about was the pressing deadlines that he had left behind. Phone calls to return. Projects to complete. Assignments to finish. Meetings to make.

Years later, their two diaries were discovered as each recorded what the day had meant to them. In the father's journal was recorded, "Took my son fishing. Another day lost." But in the boy's diary, the entry read, "Spent the day with dad. It was one of the greatest days of my life."

THE NEGATIVE NEIGHBOR

CHARLES SWINDOLL

FROM *THREE STEPS FORWARD, TWO STEPS BACK*

I once heard about a farmer who was continually optimistic, seldom discouraged or blue. He had a neighbor who was just the opposite. Grim and gloomy, he faced each new morning with a heavy sigh.

The happy, optimistic farmer would see the sun coming up and shout over the roar of the tractor, "Look at that beautiful sun and the clear sky!" And with a frown, the negative neighbor would reply, "Yeah—it'll probably scorch the crops!"

When clouds would gather and much-needed rain would start to fall, our positive friend would smile across the fence, "Ain't this great— God is giving our corn a drink today!" Again, the same negative response, "Uh huh...but if it doesn't stop 'fore long it'll flood and wash everything away."

One day the optimist decided to put his pessimistic neighbor to the maximum test. He bought the smartest, most expensive bird dog he could find. He trained him to do things no other dog on earth could do—impossible feats that would surely astound anyone.

He invited the pessimist to go duck hunting with him. They sat in the boat, hidden in the duck blind. In came the ducks. Both men fired and several ducks fell into the water. "Go get 'em!" ordered the owner with a gleam in his eye. The dog leaped out of the boat, walked on the water, and picked up the birds one by one.

"Well, what do ya think of that?"

Unsmiling, the pessimist answered, "He can't swim, can he?"

LADDER OF SUCCESS

There are four rungs on the ladder of success:
Plan Purposefully
Prepare Prayerfully
Proceed Positively
Pursue Persistently

African-American proverb

ENCOURAGEMENT

EVERY MINUTE

Perhaps once in a hundred years
a person may be ruined
by excessive praise,
But surely once every minute
someone dies inside for lack of it.

CECIL G. OSBORNE

COMING HOME

DAVID REDDING

FROM *JESUS MAKES ME LAUGH*

I remember going home from the Navy for the first time during World War II. Home was so far out in the country that when we went hunting we had to go toward town. We had moved there for my father's health when I was just 13. We raised cattle and sheep.

I started a little flock of Shropshire sheep, the kind that are completely covered by wool except for a black nose and the tips of black legs. My father helped them have their twins at lambing time, and I could tell each one of the flock apart at a distance with no trouble. I had a beautiful ram. Next door was a poor man who had a beautiful dog and a small flock of sheep he wanted to improve with my ram. He asked me if he could borrow the ram; in return he would let me have the choice of the litter from his prize dog.

That is how I got Teddy, a big, black Scottish shepherd. Teddy was my dog, and he would do anything for me. He waited for me to come home from school. He slept beside me, and when I whistled he ran to me even if he were eating. At night no one could get within a half mile without Teddy's permission. During those long summers in the fields I would only see the family at night, but Teddy was with me all the time. And so when I went away to war, I didn't know how to leave him. How do you explain to someone who loves you that you are leaving him and will not be chasing woodchucks with him tomorrow like always?

So, coming home that first time from the Navy was something I can scarcely describe. The last bus stop was fourteen miles from the farm. I got off there that night at about eleven o'clock and walked the rest of the way home. It was two or three in the morning before I was within a half mile of the house. It was pitch dark, but I knew every step of the way. Suddenly Teddy heard me and began his warning bark. Then I whistled only once. The barking stopped. There was a yelp of recognition, and I knew that a big black form was hurtling toward me in the darkness. Almost immediately he was there in my arms. To this day that is the best way I can explain what I mean by coming home.

What comes home to me now is the eloquence with which that unforgettable memory speaks to me of my God. If my dog, without any explanation, would love me and take me back after all that time, wouldn't my God?

JIMMY DURANTE

TIM HANSEL

FROM *HOLY SWEAT*

There's a wonderful story about Jimmy Durante, one of the great entertainers of a generation ago. He was asked to be a part of a show for World War II veterans. He told them his schedule was very busy and he could afford only a few minutes, but if they wouldn't mind his doing one short monologue and immediately leaving for his next appointment, he would come. Of course, the show's director agreed happily.

But when Jimmy got on stage, something interesting happened. He went through the short monologue and then stayed. The applause grew louder and louder and he kept staying. Pretty soon, he had been on fifteen, twenty, then thirty minutes. Finally, he took a last bow and left the stage. Backstage someone stopped him and said, "I thought you had to go after a few minutes. What happened?"

Jimmy answered, "I did have to go, but I can show you the reason I stayed. You can see for yourself if you'll look on the front row." In the front row were two men, each of whom had lost an arm in the war. One had lost his right arm and the other had lost his left. Together, they were able to clap, and that's exactly what they were doing, loudly and cheerfully.

OUR FRIENDSHIP TREE

HARRISON KELLY

Friendships that last longest are the ones with the deepest roots. Those are the ones that mature into brotherhood.

In the third grade, I was still the new kid in school, only with a year's experience. Just twelve months before, my family moved into a suburb of Memphis named Frayser, a middle-class neighborhood instilled with a strong work ethic. But the residents were a little hesitant when it came to outsiders.

One day, a boy with a nervous look on his face came into our class for the first time. His name was Tom and his family had just moved from Nashville. You could tell he didn't like being the new kid, no more than I did.

Since the desk behind mine was the only one empty, the teacher assigned it to him. Knowing firsthand of the difficulty in getting to know people, I made the first effort. Soon we became best friends, a camaraderie that outlasted classes well into the summer.

Tom's house was a mile and a half from mine, near a large townhouse development in one of the quieter sections. I lived on the boulevard with its non-stop hurry. Even though we lived so far apart, our friendship grew.

We'd meet each other half-way, under a yellow oak that hung over the parking lot of the local Methodist church. The tree's mammoth size was legendary with a trunk at least six feet around and branches as big as barrels. We called it Our Friendship Tree as it seemed to symbolize everything we felt about our mutual esteem.

It was a stopping point, a meeting place, a beginning and an ending. During that first summer, we met there, with baseball gloves in hand to plan our mornings and would depart every afternoon, resolved to return.

As the years marched before our eyes, it seemed like Our Friendship Tree was always there, watching our growth, guiding our paths. We walked under its orange leaves to Cub Scouts in the fall and first talked about girls while resting at the foot of its trunk. We met under its branches in tuxedos the night of our senior prom. When we wore our caps and gowns at our baccalaureate. Again, as we threw rice after our weddings. That tree seemed to be as much a part of our lives as the friendship itself.

As we became adults and parents, we moved away from Frayser. However, we still kept in touch with each other. One day, Tom called me out of the blue. He told me that lightning had struck Our Friendship Tree and had caused it to fall to the ground. I shed a tear as I realized its roots were really ours. Gone was a symbol of our childhood together, something never to be replaced.

Six months passed, then I read in the newspaper about a man that made writing pens from wood that had special meanings. As I read the article, I wished that I would have saved a piece from Our Friendship Tree. But as I read further, to my surprise, the man lived in Frayser! Maybe he had some wood from that old tree?

Sure enough, he did. The tree grew on the property of his old church and he had made pens for some in the congregation. When he said he had two pens left, I almost couldn't hold myself back.

I met Tom for lunch one afternoon and gave him one of the pens, as a symbol of our past and a promise to always be there in the future. I kept the other for myself and often reflect as I write, remembering my roots.

THE POLICEMAN
AND THE TOWELS

CHRISTOPHER DE VINCK

FROM *SIMPLE WONDERS*

I was home alone with the children: five-year-old David, three-year-old Karen, and Michael, the infant. Roe was at work, her two-night-a-week position as a receptionist for an orthodontist. Just before dinner I noticed Karen had a high fever. *Perhaps I should take her to the doctor,* I thought. Roe agreed, for I had called her at work. After I hung up the phone, I walked out of the kitchen and found Karen slumped on the living room couch. She was facing the ceiling and foaming at the mouth. Her eyes were rolled back. She was still and unconscious. I thought she was dying.

I didn't know what to do. Michael wasn't walking yet. David was bewildered. I simply wanted to run into the street and scream for help. I did scream: "Karen! Karen!" She wasn't responding.

The telephone. I called the police, the ambulance.

I rushed about through the dining room, through the living room, holding Karen, calling her name again and again, but there was still no response.

A minute later, I called the police again. "Please hurry!" Before I could place the receiver back in its place, the doorbell rang. Red and blue lights flashed throughout the neighborhood. I quickly answered the solid knocking, and there, before me, stood the tallest, broadest giant of a policeman I had ever seen. I could smell his leather coat. His shoes were shined.

"I don't know what happened to my daughter! She isn't responding!"

"She's having a seizure," the policeman said in a low, confident voice. "Is she ill?"

"She has a fever! I know that! I was about to call the doctor!"

The policeman peacefully entered the house. "Let's run some cool water in the bathtub. We need to bring her fever down."

I pointed to the stairs. The policeman walked up, entered the bathroom, and began running water. I was not aware that three or four neighbors had entered the house and were tending to David and Michael. I was not aware that the ambulance was on its way. All I knew was that a stranger was lifting my daughter out of my arms and gently placing her in a tepid tub of water.

I knelt on the floor to the left of the policeman. He, too, was kneeling and leaning over the side of the bathtub, scooping up handfuls of water and slowly pouring them over Karen's hot back. His gun was belted to his waist. His badge scraped against the porcelain.

As he was tending to Karen, he turned to me and whispered, "I have a three-year-old daughter, too."

Karen began to respond. I dried her with a towel, dropped it on the floor, and wrapped her in a wool blanket, and carried her downstairs. My neighbors said they would watch the boys. The ambulance drove onto the front lawn and right up to the front door. Two-way radios squawked in the background.

I stepped into the ambulance with Karen, through that wide, rear door, and held her against my chest. I cried and cried.

The emergency room doctor said that Karen had suffered a febrile seizure, which some young children are prone to—a consultation with our family doctor was suggested. Her temperature dropped. Karen was fine.

In Tennessee Williams's play, *The Glass Menagerie,* Amanda, the mother, tells her son, "We have to do all that we can to build ourselves up. In these trying times we live in, all that we have to cling to is each other."

After my daughter was safely tucked in bed that night, as I walked past the bathroom I noticed that our policeman had drained the bathtub and folded the towels.

This policeman, my policeman, had no reason to be so kind, so interested, so caring, but like the good Samaritan, he stopped and felt compassion for me and for my daughter.

Jesus told the story about the Samaritan because he wanted to give an example of the type of people who will be rewarded eternal peace in heaven: those who love their neighbors for no reward.

MAKING FRIENDS

You can make more friends in two months by becoming genuinely interested in other people than you can in two years by trying to get other people interested in you.

DALE CARNEGIE

COSTLY ERROR

AUTHOR UNKNOWN

FROM *MORE OF...THE BEST OF BITS & PIECES*

Many years ago a senior executive of the then Standard Oil Company made a wrong decision that cost the company more than $2 million. John D. Rockefeller was then running the company. On the day the news leaked out, most of the executives of the company were finding various ingenious ways of avoiding Rockefeller, lest his wrath descend on their heads.

There was one exception, however; he was Edward T. Bedford, a partner in the company. Bedford was scheduled to see Rockefeller that day, and he kept the appointment, even though he was prepared to listen to a long harangue against the man who made the error in judgment.

When Bedford entered the office, the powerful head of the gigantic Standard Oil empire was bent over his desk busily writing with a pencil on a pad of paper. Bedford stood silently, not wishing to interrupt. After a few minutes Rockefeller looked up.

"Oh, it's you, Bedford," he said calmly. "I suppose you've heard about our loss?"

Bedford said that he had.

"I've been thinking it over," Rockefeller said, "and before I ask the man to discuss the matter, I've been making some notes."

Bedford later told the story this way:

"Across the top of the page was written, 'Points in favor of Mr. _____.' There followed a long list of the man's virtues, including a brief description of how he had helped the company make the right decision on three separate occasions that had earned many times the cost of his recent error.

"I never forgot that lesson. In later years, whenever I was tempted to rip into anyone, I forced myself first to sit down and thoughtfully compile as long a list of good points as I possibly could. Invariably, by the time I finished my inventory, I would see the matter in its true perspective and keep my temper under control. There is no telling how many times this habit has prevented me from committing one of the costliest mistakes any executive can make—*losing his temper.*

"I commend it to anyone who must deal with people."

AN IMPORTANT LESSON

RABBI HAROLD S. KUSHNER

I was sitting on a beach one summer day, watching two children, a boy and a girl, playing in the sand. They were hard at work, by the water's edge, building an elaborate sand castle with gates and towers and moats and internal passages.

Just when they had nearly finished their project, a big wave came along and knocked it down, reducing it to a heap of wet sand. I expected the children to burst into tears, devastated by what had happened to all their hard work.

But they surprised me. Instead, they ran up the shore away from the water, laughing and holding hands, and sat down to build another castle. I realized that they had taught me an important lesson. All the things in our lives, all the complicated structures we spend so much time and energy creating, are built on sand. Only our relationships to other people endure. Sooner or later, the wave will come along and knock down what we have worked so hard to build up. When that happens, only the person who has somebody's hand to hold will be able to laugh.

ENCOURAGING WORDS

BARBARA JOHNSON

FROM *WE BRAKE FOR JOY!*

Someone has said that encouragement is simply reminding a person of the "shoulders" he's standing on, the heritage he's been given. That's what happened when a young man, the son of a star baseball player, was drafted by one of the minor league teams. As hard as he tried, his first season was disappointing, and by midseason he expected to be released any day.

The coaches were bewildered by his failure because he possessed all the characteristics of a superb athlete, but he couldn't seem to incorporate those advantages into a coordinated effort. He seemed to have become disconnected from his potential.

His future seemed darkest one day when he had already struck out his first time at bat. Then he stepped up to the batter's box again and quickly ran up two strikes. The catcher called a time-out and trotted to the pitcher's mound for a conference. While they were busy, the umpire, standing behind the plate, spoke casually to the boy.

Then play resumed, the next pitch was thrown—and the young man knocked it out of the park. That was the turning point. From then on, he played the game with a new confidence and power that quickly drew the attention of the parent team, and he was called up to the majors.

On the day he was leaving for the city, one of his coaches asked him what had caused such a turnaround. The young man replied it was the encouraging remark the umpire had made that day when his baseball career had seemed doomed.

"He told me I reminded him of all the times he had stood behind my dad in the batter's box," the boy explained. "He said I was holding the bat just the way Dad had held it. And he told me, 'I can see his genes in you; you have your father's arms.' After that, whenever I swung the bat, I just imagined I was using Dad's arms instead of my own."

BLESSED

*Blessed are they who have the gift
of making friends, for it is one of God's best gifts.
It involves many things, but above all,
the power of going out of one's self
and appreciating whatever is noble
and loving in another.*

THOMAS HUGHES

READING
BETWEEN THE LINES

AUTHOR UNKNOWN

Dear Dad,

$chool i$ really great. I am making lot$ of friend$ and $tudying very hard. With all my $tuff, I $imply can't think of anything I need, $o if you would like, you can ju$t $end me a card, a$ I would love to hear from you.

Love,

Your Daughter $u$an

Dear $u$an,

I kNOw that astroNOmy, ecoNOmics, and oceaNOgraphy are eNOugh to keep even an hoNOr student busy. Do NOt forget that the pursuit of kNOwldege is a NOble task, and you can never study eNOugh.

Love,

Dad

MY NAME IS IKE

GARY PAULSEN

FROM *MY LIFE IN DOG YEARS*

M uch of my childhood in Thief River Falls, Minn., was excruciatingly lonely. Family troubles, devastating shyness and a complete lack of social skills ensured a life of solitude. Hunting was not only my opening into a world of wonder, it was my salvation.

From the age of 12, I lived, breathed, existed to hunt and fish. On school days I would hunt in the morning and evening. On Fridays I would head into the woods, often for the entire weekend.

Still, I had not learned to love solitude as I do now. I would see something beautiful—the sun through the leaves; a deer moving through dappled light—and I would want to point and say to someone, "Look!" But there was no one there.

Then I met Ike.

It was the beginning of duck season. I got up at 3 A.M. and walked from our apartment four blocks to the railroad yard, then across the Eighth Street bridge. There I dropped to the riverbank and started walking along the water into the woods.

In the dark it was hard going. After a mile and a half I was wading in swamp muck and went to pull myself up the bank to harder ground.

The mud was as slick as grease. I fell, then scrabbled up the bank again, shotgun in one hand and grabbing at roots with the other. I had just gained the top when a part of the darkness detached itself, leaned close to my face and went "woof."

Not "arf" or "ruff" or a growl, but "woof."

For half a second I froze. Then I let go of the shrub and fell back down the incline. On the way down the thought hit: bear.

I clawed at my pockets for shells and inserted one into my shotgun. I was aiming when something about the shape stopped me.

Whatever it was had remained sitting at the top of the bank, looking down at me. There was just enough dawn to show a silhouette. It was a dog. A big dog, a black dog, but a dog.

I lowered the gun and wiped the mud out of my eyes. "Who owns you?" I asked. The dog didn't move, and I climbed the bank again. "Hello!" I called into the woods. "I have your dog here!"

There was nobody.

"So you're a stray." But strays were shy and usually starved; this dog, a Labrador, was well-fed and his coat was thick. He stayed near me.

"Well," I said. "What do I do with you?" On impulse I added, "You want to hunt?"

He knew that word. His tail hammered the ground and he wiggled, then moved off along the river.

I had never hunted with a dog before, but I started to follow. It was light enough now to shoot, so I kept the gun ready. We had not gone 50 yards when two mallards exploded out of some thick grass near the bank and started across the river.

I raised the gun, cocked it, aimed just above the right-hand duck and squeezed the trigger. There was a crash, and the duck fell into the water.

When I shot ducks over the river before, I had to wait for the current to bring the body to shore. This time was different. With the smell of the powder still in the air, the dog was off the bank in a great leap. He hit the water swimming, his shoulders pumping as he churned the surface in a straight line to the dead duck. He took it gently in his mouth, turned and swam back. Climbing the bank, he put the duck by my right foot, then moved off a couple of feet and sat.

It was fully light now, and I could see that the dog had a collar and tag. I petted him—he let me, in a reserved way—and pulled his tag to the side to read it.

My name is Ike.

That's all it said. No address, no owner's name.

"Well, Ike"—his tail wagged—"I'd like to thank you for bringing me the duck."

And that was how it started.

For the rest of the season, I hunted the river early every morning. I'd come across the bridge, start down the river and Ike would be there. By the middle of the second week, I felt as if we'd been hunting with each other forever.

When the hunting was done, he'd trot back with me until we arrived at the bridge. There he would sit, and nothing I did would make him come farther.

I tried waiting to see where he would go, but when it was obvious I wasn't going to leave, he merely lay down and went to sleep. Once I left him, crossed the bridge and then hid in back of a building to watch. He stayed until I was out of sight, then turned and trotted north along the river and into the woods.

If the rest of his life was a mystery, when we were together we became fast friends. I'd cook an extra egg sandwich for him, and when there were no ducks, we would talk. That is, I would talk. Ike would sit, his enormous head resting on my knee, his huge brown eyes looking up at me while I petted him and told him of all my troubles.

On the weekends when I stayed out, I would construct a lean-to and make a fire. Ike would curl up on the edge of my blanket. Many mornings I'd awaken to find him under the frost-covered blanket with me, his breath rumbling against my side.

It seemed Ike had always been in my life. Then one morning he wasn't there. I would wait in the mornings by the bridge, but he never showed again. I thought he might have been hit by a car or his owners might have moved away. But I could not learn more of him. I mourned him and missed him.

I grew and went into the crazy parts of my life, the mistakes a young man could make. Later I got back into dogs, sled dogs, and ran the Iditarod race across Alaska.

After my first run I came back home to Minnesota with slides of the race. A sporting goods store in Bemidji had been one of my sponsors, and one evening I gave a public slide show.

There was an older man sitting in a wheelchair, and I saw that when I told how Cookie, my lead dog, had saved my life, his eyes teared up and he nodded.

When the event was over, he wheeled up and shook my hand.

"I had a dog like your Cookie—a dog that saved my life."

"Oh, did you run sleds?"

He shook his head. "No, not like that. I lived up in Thief River Falls when I was drafted to serve in the Korean War. I had a Labrador retriever that I raised and hunted with. Then I was wounded—lost the use of my legs. When I came back from the hospital, he was waiting. He spent the rest of his life by my side.

"I would have gone crazy without him. I'd sit for hours and talk to him..." He faded off, and his eyes were moist again. "I still miss him."

I looked at him, then out the store window. It was spring and the snow was melting outside, but I was seeing a 13-year-old and a Lab sitting in a duck blind in the fall.

Thief River Falls, he said—and the Korean War. The time was right, and the place.

"Your dog," I said. "Was he named Ike?"

The man smiled and nodded. "Why, yes. But how...Did you know him?"

That was why Ike had not come back. He had another job.

"Yes," I said, turning to him. "He was my friend."

WHAT KIDS NEED

MARTY WILKINS

Today's kids desperately need heroes who…

...play catch, enjoy tea parties or wrestle because the heart of a child is there and they set out to capture it.

...laugh till their belly hurts and tears fall from their eyes while secretly creating deep friendships and memories that last a lifetime.

...make mistakes but consider them to be wonderful opportunities to learn.

...place an out of tune preschool concert or a ten-year-old's baseball game on life's agenda because they are of infinite worth to those playing.

...love at all times, because love is a gift freely given and not a reward for service well done.

...listen eye to eye and with both ears even if it means getting on one knee.

...admit when they are wrong and work to make things right.

…hear about those in need and say, "Let's do something to help right now!" and set off an uncontrollable wildfire of generosity and kindness.

…give the credit to others and empower those they touch to succeed in all that they do.

…model love as action, commitment and truth even when it hurts because they believe God can work miracles in even the hardest heart.

…love the Lord with all their heart, soul, and mind and know that the rest is just details.

THE GREATEST ASSET

I consider my ability to arouse enthusiasm among the men the greatest asset I possess, and the way to develop the best that is in a man is by appreciation and encouragement. There is nothing else that so kills the ambitions of man as criticisms from his superiors. I never criticize anyone. I believe in giving a man incentive to work. So I am anxious to praise but loath to find fault. If I like anything, I am hearty in my approbation and lavish in my praise.

CHARLES SCHWAB

LONGER,
DADDY...LONGER

GARY SMALLEY AND JOHN TRENT

FROM *LEAVING THE LIGHT ON*

Recently, a woman grabbed my arm at a conference after I had finished speaking on the enormous need we all have for affirmation.

"Dr. Trent, may I tell you my story?" she asked. "Actually, it's a story of something my son did with my granddaughter that illustrates what you've been talking about—the importance of affirmation.

"My son has two daughters, one who's five and one who is in the 'terrible twos.'" When a grandmother says this child is in the "terrible twos," believe me, she is!

"For several years, my son has taken the oldest girl out for a 'date' time, but he had never taken the two-year-old until recently. On his first 'date' with the younger one, he took her out to breakfast at a local fast food restaurant.

"They had just gotten their pancakes and my son decided it would be a good time to tell this child how much he loved and appreciated her."

"Jenny," her son had said, "I want you to know how much I love you, and how special you are to Mom and me. We prayed for you for years, and now that you're here and growing up to be such a wonderful girl, we couldn't be more proud of you."

Once he had said all this, he stopped talking and reached over for his fork to begin eating...but he never got the fork to his mouth.

His daughter reached out her little hand and laid it on her father's hand. His eyes went to hers, and in a soft, pleading voice she said, "Longer, Daddy...longer."

He put down his fork and proceeded to tell her some more reasons and ways they loved and appreciated her, and then he again reached for his fork. A second time...and a third...and a fourth time he heard the words, "Longer, Daddy...longer."

This father never did get much to eat that morning, but his daughter got the emotional nourishment she needed so much. In fact, a few days later, she spontaneously ran up to her mother and said, "I'm a really special daughter, Mommy. Daddy told me so."

GRADUATION SPEECH

TIM WILDMON

RETOLD BY ALICE GRAY

They walked in tandem, each of the ninety-three students filing into the already crowded auditorium. With rich maroon gowns flowing and the traditional tasseled caps, they looked almost as grown up as they felt. Dads swallowed hard behind broad smiles, and moms freely brushed away tears.

This class would not pray during the commencement—not by choice but because of a recent court ruling that prohibited it. The principal and several students were careful to stay within the guidelines allowed by the ruling. They gave inspirational and challenging speeches, but no one mentioned divine guidance and no one asked for blessings on the graduates or their families. The speeches were nice, but they were fairly routine.

Until the final speech received a standing ovation.

A solitary student walked proudly to the microphone. He stood still and silent for just a moment, and then he delivered his speech—a resounding sneeze. The rest of the students rose immediately to their feet, and in unison they said, "God bless you."

The audience exploded in applause. This graduating class found a unique way to invoke God's blessings on their future—with or without the court's approval.

CELEBRATE THE MOMENTS OF YOUR LIFE

GARY SMALLEY

FROM *LOVE IS A DECISION*

Those who are wise romantics will realize that some special date or event every year can be used to fan the romantic flame. I recall one man, who did put together a very special celebration for his wife to honor her for a sacrifice she had made for him.

It was the eve of his graduation from a long, grueling master's degree program. Four years of intensive, full-time study had finally found him about to receive his diploma.

His wife planned a special party where many of their friends were to come and help him celebrate the long awaited "day of deliverance." There would be cake, refreshments, banners, streamers, a pool nearby, croquet, and other yard games. Many people had already accepted her invitation to come, and it looked like it would be a full house. Her husband, though, had other ideas. He secretly contacted each person who had received an invitation and told them he wanted to make the party a surprise in honor of *her.* Yes, there would be banners, streamers, and all the rest, but they would bear her name, not his.

He wanted to do something special to let her know how much he appreciated the years of sacrifice she'd devoted to his graduation. Working full time to put him through, and putting off her dreams of a house and family, had, in many ways, been harder on her than the long hours of study had been on him.

When the day arrived, she was busy with preparations and last minute details, still convinced that all was going according to plan. He arranged to get her away from the party site, and while she was gone, he put up a huge banner with her name on it. During that time all the guests arrived as well.

She returned to be greeted with a huge "SURPRISE!!!" and when she realized what was going on, she could barely fight back the tears. Her husband asked a few people to share what they most appreciated about her. Then he stood before them and, with tender words of love and appreciation, expressed his gratitude for all she'd done for him. When he was through, they saluted her with an iced-tea toast.

The rest of the evening was a fun-filled fiesta of laughing, catching up with one another, water volleyball, yard games, and more food than anyone could eat. It was a celebration of an experience they both shared, and by commemorating it in a special way, this husband created a lifelong, romantic memorial to his wife's love and dedication.

DO YOU KNOW WHO HIS DADDY IS?

ZIG ZIGLAR

FROM *OVER THE TOP*

I n his beautiful book *Rising above the Crowd,* Brian Harbour tells the story of Ben Hooper. When Ben Hooper was born many years ago in the foothills of East Tennessee, little boys and girls like Ben who were born to unwed mothers were ostracized and treated terribly. By the time he was three years old, the other children would scarcely play with him. Parents were saying idiotic things like, "What's a boy like that doing playing with our children?" as if the child had anything at all to do with his own birth.

Saturday was the toughest day of all. Ben's mom would take him down to the little general store to buy their supplies for the week. Invariably, the other parents in the store would make caustic remarks just loudly enough for both mother and child to hear, comments like, "Did you ever figure out who his daddy is?" What a tough, tough childhood.

In those days there was no kindergarten. So, at age six, little Ben entered the first grade. He was given his own desk, as were all the children. At recess, he stayed at that little desk and studied because none of the other children would play with him. At noon, little Ben could be found eating his sack lunch all alone. The happy chatter of the children who shunned him was barely audible from where he sat.

It was a big event when anything changed in the foothills of East Tennessee, and when little Ben was twelve years old a new preacher came to pastor the little church in Ben's town.

Almost immediately, little Ben started hearing exciting things about him—about how loving and nonjudgmental he was. How he accepted people just as they were, and when he was with them, he made them feel like the most important people in the world. Reportedly, the preacher had charisma. When he walked into a group of any size, anywhere, the entire complexion of that group changed. Their smiles broadened, their laughter increased, and their spirits rose.

One Sunday, though he had never been to church a day in his life, little Ben Hooper decided he was going to go and hear the preacher. He got there late and he left early because he did not want to attract any attention, but he liked what he heard. For the first time in that young boy's life, he caught just a glimmer of hope.

Ben was back in church the next Sunday and the next and the next. He always got there late and always left early, but his hope was building each Sunday.

On about the sixth or seventh Sunday the message was so moving and exciting that Ben became absolutely enthralled with it. It was almost as if there were a sign behind the preacher's head that read, "For you, little Ben Hooper of unknown parentage, there is hope!" Ben got so wrapped up in the message, he forgot about the time and didn't notice that a number of people had come in after he had taken his seat.

Suddenly, the services were over. Ben very quickly stood up to leave as he had in all the Sundays past, but the aisles were clogged with people and he could not run out. As he was working his way through the crowd, he felt a hand on his shoulder. He turned around and looked up, right into the eyes of the young preacher who asked him a question that had been on the mind of every person there for the last twelve years: "Whose boy are you?"

Instantly, the church grew deathly quiet. Slowly, a smile started to spread across the face of the young preacher until it broke into a huge grin, and he exclaimed, "Oh! I know whose boy you are! Why, the family resemblance is unmistakable. You are a child of God!"

And with that the young preacher swatted him across the rear and said, "That's quite a heritage you've got there, boy! Now, go and see to it that you live up to it."

A friend is one who walks in when others walk out.

WALTER WINCHELL

FATHERHOOD

MAGICAL MOMENT

After getting my first chance to change your diaper, I brought you back down-stairs. I turned on the television, and as luck would have it, the San Francisco 49ers were playing.... I turned out all the lights, lay down on the couch, and put you on my chest. I was so afraid that my big hands were going to drop you, but I held on. It wasn't five minutes later that you fell asleep, holding my finger.... It was at that moment I realized that I was a dad.

JOHN BARNET

FROM *PARENTS* MAGAZINE

THROUGH THE DARKNESS

JAMES C. DOBSON

FROM *HOME WITH A HEART*

I'm told that when I was a very small child—maybe two years of age—my family lived in a one-bedroom apartment, and my little bed was located beside the bed of my parents. My father said that it was common during that time to awaken at night to a little voice that was whispering, "Daddy? Daddy? Daddy?"

My father would answer quietly, "What, Jimmy?"

And I would say, "Hold my hand!"

My dad would reach across the darkness and grope for my little hand, finally engulfing it in his. He said later that the instant he had my hand firmly in his grip, my arm would become limp and my breathing deep and regular. I would immediately fall back to sleep.

You see, I only wanted to know that he was there! Until the day he died, I continued to reach for him—for his assurance, for his guidance—but mostly just to know that he was there.

Then, so very quickly, I found myself in my dad's place. And I wanted to be there for my children—not just a name on their birth certificate, but a strong, warm, and loving presence in their lives.

You see, a dad occupies a place in a child's heart that no one else can satisfy. So to all the men out there who are blessed to be called fathers: I urge you to be there for the little ones in your life who call you "Dad."

WHEN GOD CREATED FATHERS

ERMA BOMBECK

FROM *FOREVER, ERMA*

When the good Lord was creating fathers, He started with a tall frame.

A female angel nearby said, "What kind of father is that? If you're going to make children so close to the ground, why have you put fathers up so high? He won't be able to shoot marbles without kneeling, tuck a child in bed without bending or even kiss a child without a lot of stooping."

...And God smiled and said, "Yes, but if I make him child-size, who would children have to look up to?"

And when God made a father's hands, they were large and sinewy.

The angel shook her head sadly and said, "Large hands are clumsy. They can't manage diaper pins, small buttons, rubber bands on ponytails or even remove splinters caused by baseball bats."

And God smiled and said, "I know, but they're large enough to hold everything a small boy empties from his pockets at the end of a day, yet small enough to cup a child's face."

And then God molded long, slim legs and broad shoulders.

The angel nearly had a heart attack. "Boy, this is the end of the week, all right," she clucked. "Do you realize you just made a father without a lap? How is he going to pull a child close to him without the kid falling between his legs?"

And God smiled and said, "A mother needs a lap. A father needs strong shoulders to pull a sled, balance a boy on a bicycle or hold a sleepy head on the way home from the circus."

God was in the middle of creating two of the largest feet anyone had ever seen when the angel could contain herself no longer. "That's not fair. Do you honestly think those large boats are going to dig out of bed early in the morning when the baby cries? Or walk through a small birthday party without crushing at least three of the guests?"

And God smiled and said, "They'll work. You'll see. They'll support a small child who wants to ride a horse to Banbury Cross or scare off mice at the summer cabin or display shoes that will be a challenge to fill."

God worked throughout the night, giving the father few words but a firm, authoritative voice and eyes that saw everything but remained calm and tolerant.

Finally, almost as an afterthought, He added tears. Then He turned to the angel and said, "Now, are you satisfied that he can love as much as a mother?"

The angel shutteth up.

A FATHER'S PROMISE

ARTHUR GORDON

FROM *COACHING CHAMPIONS*

When I was around 13 and my brother was 10, Father promised to take us to the circus. But at lunch there was a phone call; some urgent business required his attention downtown. My brother and I braced ourselves for the disappointment. Then we heard him say, "No, I won't be down. It will have to wait."

When he came back to the table, Mother smiled. "The circus keeps coming back, you know."

"I know," said Father, "but childhood doesn't."

WAKE-UP CALL

BOB WELCH

FROM *A FATHER FOR ALL SEASONS*

I was sitting in a bathtub full of moldy sheetrock when my 13-year-old son asked the question. "Can you take me golfing sometime?" he said.

I had a bathroom to remodel. It was fall, and the forecast for the next week was for 100 percent chance of Oregon's liquid sunshine. I wanted to say no. "Sure," I said. "What did you have in mind?"

"Well, maybe you could, like, pick up Jared and me after school on Friday and take us out to Oakway."

"Sounds good."

Friday came. The showers continued. Looking out the window, moldy sheetrock seemed the saner choice. But at the appointed hour, I changed from home-improvement garb to rain-protection garb and loaded the boys' clubs and mine in the back of the car. In front of the school, Ryan and Jared piled in. Ryan looked at me with a perplexed expression.

"What's with the golf hat, Dad?" he said.

It was, I thought, a silly question, like asking a scuba diver what's with the swim fins.

"Well, I thought we were going to play some golf."

A peculiar pause ensued, like a phone line temporarily gone dead.

"Uh, you're going, *too?*" he asked.

Suddenly, it struck me like a three-iron to my gut: I hadn't been invited.

Thirteen years of parenting flashed before my eyes. The birth. The diapers. The late-night feedings. Helping with homework. Building forts. Fixing bikes. Going to games. Going camping. Going everywhere together—my son and I.

Now I hadn't been invited. This was it. This was the end of our relationship as I had always known it. This was "Adios, Old Man, thanks for the memories but I'm old enough to swing my own clubs now, so go back to your rocking chair and crossword puzzles and—oh yeah—here's a half-off coupon for your next bottle of Geritol."

All these memories sped by in about two seconds, leaving me about three seconds to respond before Ryan would get suspicious and think I had actually expected to be playing golf with him and his friend.

I had to say something. I wanted to say this: *How could you do this to me? Throw me overboard like unused crab bait?* We had always been a team. But this was abandonment. Adult abuse.

This was Lewis turning to Clark in 1805 and saying: "Later, Bill. I can make it the rest of the way to Oregon without you." John Glenn radioing Mission Control to say, thanks, but he could take it from here. Simon bailing out on Garfunkel during "Bridge Over Troubled Water."

Why did it all have to change?

Enough of this mind-wandering. I needed to level with him. I needed to express how hurt I was. Share my gut-level feelings. Muster all the courage I could find, bite the bullet, and spill my soul.

So I said, "Me? Play? Naw. You know I'm up to my ears in the remodel project."

We drove on in silence for a few moments. "So, how are you planning to pay for this?" I asked, my wounded ego reaching for the dagger.

"Uh, could you loan me seven dollars?"

Oh, I get it. He doesn't want *me*, but he'll gladly take my *money*.

"No problem," I said.

I dropped him and Jared off, wished them luck, and headed for home. My son was on his own now. Nobody there to tell him how to fade a five-iron, how to play that tricky downhiller, how to hit the sand shot. And what if there's lightning? What about hypothermia? A runaway golf cart? A band of militant gophers? He's so small. Who would take care of him?

There I was, alone, driving away from him. Not just for now. Forever. This was it. The bond was broken. Life would never be the same.

I walked in the door. "What are you doing home?" my wife asked.

I knew it would sound like some 13-year-old who was the only one in the gang not invited to the slumber party, but maintaining my immature demur, I said it anyway.

"I wasn't *invited*," I replied, with a trace of snottiness.

Another one of those peculiar pauses ensued. Then my wife laughed. Out loud. At first I was hurt. Then I, too, laughed, the situation suddenly becoming much clearer.

I went back to the bathroom remodel and began realizing that this is what life is all about: change. This is what father and sons must ultimately do: change. This is what I've been preparing him for since he first looked at me and screamed in terror: not to play golf without me, but to take on the world without me. With his own set of clubs. His own game plan. His own faith.

God was remodeling my son. Adding some space here. Putting in a new feature there. In short, allowing him to become more than he could ever be if I continued to hover over him. Just like when I was a kid and, at Ryan's age, I would sling my plaid golf bag over my shoulder and ride my bike five miles across town to play golf at a small public course called Marysville that I imagined as Augusta National.

I remember how grown-up I felt, walking into that dark clubhouse, the smoke rising from the poker game off to the left, and proudly pluncking down my two dollars for nine holes. Would I have wanted my father there with me that day? Naw. A boy's gotta do what a boy's gotta do: grow up.

I went back to the bathroom remodel project. A few hours later, I heard Ryan walk in the front door. I heard him complain to his mother that his putts wouldn't drop, that his drives were slicing, and that the course was like a lake. He sounded like someone I knew. His tennis shoes squeaked with water as I heard him walk back to where I was working on the bathroom.

"Dad," he said, dripping on the floor, "my game stinks. Can you take me golfing sometime? I need some help."

I wanted to hug him. Rev my radial-arm saw in celebration. Shout: "I'm still needed!" I wanted to tell God, "Thanks for letting me be part of this kid's remodel job."

Instead, I got one of those serious-dad looks on my face and stoically said, "Sure, Ry, anytime."

Fathers are what give daughters away to other men who aren't nearly good enough...so they can have grandchildren that are smarter than anybody's.

PAUL HARVEY

CAR TRIP

PAUL HARVEY

FROM *PAUL HARVEY'S FOR WHAT IT'S WORTH*

The Bartons of Sacramento were driving toward home in dark rain with the parents in the front seat and their two little girls in the rear. After a hundred miles of freeway, they turned off on the last twenty miles of winding country road. Suddenly they were confronted by another car's blinding headlights. The other car was coming over the crest of a hill. Mr. Barton saw the oncoming glare through his wet windshield and swerved off the road onto a muddy shoulder. The car spun wildly in a circle, then fishtailed as Mr. Barton fought to gain control—and finally, facing backward, stopped.

When Eloise Barton could catch her breath, her first thought was the back seat; were her babies all right? She turned to hear her five-year-old complain, "I was asleep, Daddy. Do it again."

BRITTANY'S POEM

Dr. Steve Stephens

I t was almost ten o'clock at night and it had been a busy day.

The house was quiet—my wife was cuddled up with a good book and my children were tucked into their cozy beds. It was two weeks before Father's Day and my church had asked me to write an article on how to be a good father. I sat at my desk and scribbled a few notes.

"You ought to be...accepting," I mumbled to myself, "...and affectionate and approachable and...."

Suddenly the door to my office creaked open and 8-year-old Brittany walked in. My first reaction was to tell her to go back to bed, that it's late and she has school tomorrow. But the words I had just written stopped me, and I put my arms around her.

"Daddy, are you still writing about being a good father?"

"Yes, but I'm almost done."

"Maybe I can help you," she said, and she gently slipped a piece of paper into my hand. "It's a poem and I wrote it about you."

A FATHER'S LOVE

Fathers are kind,
Fathers are nice,
They give you hugs and kisses
right before bed.
They love you through
all the days of your life.
So what do they deserve back?
Love

I hugged my daughter and whispered, "This is the most beautiful poem I've ever read."

I held her tenderly before she went back to bed—thanking God for the privilege of being a father.

TOO BUSY

RON MEHL

FROM *GOD WORKS THE NIGHT SHIFT*

I'll never forget the day I looked out of our living room and saw Mark, our youngest, walking home from school in the driving rain. Mark was in third grade, and he was allowed to ride his bike to his grade school, located right within our subdivision. I happened to be home from the church early that day, and I was sitting in an easy chair by the window. I looked outside at the pouring rain and saw my boy in the distance, trudging his way through the downpour. His clothing was absolutely drenched and his hair was plastered against his head. I opened the door for him, and he looked up at me with a little smile, his face red from the cold.

"Hi, Dad!" he said. "You're home early."

"Hi, Son," I replied. "You're soaked to the skin."

"Yeah, I know."

"Umm, Mark, you know, if you'd ride your bike you'd get home faster. You wouldn't get so wet."

He looked at me rather sheepishly as rivulets of rain streamed from his hair down across his face. "I know, Dad."

I was puzzled. "Well, Son, if you *know*, why in the world didn't you do it?"

Then he hung his head, just a bit, and it hit me. Boy, did I feel like crawling under a table and hiding for a while. He had told me several times before that his bike had a flat tire. He had asked me, "Dad, could you please fix it for me?"

"Sure, Son," I'd promised him. "Don't worry. I'll get after it right away." But I never did. I'd forgotten all about it.

As he stood there in the entryway, dripping and shivering, he could have said, "I couldn't ride my bike today because someone promised me he'd fix it and never did." He would have had every right to say that. But he didn't. What he did say remains printed indelibly on this dad's heart.

"Aw, Dad, I know how busy you are and everything, and—I just didn't want to bother you with it again."

I thought, *Son, your dad isn't too busy; he's just too selfish.*

For me, a bike tire was no big deal—just one more thing on a long "to do" list. But for Mark, it meant more than transportation. It meant more than a long walk home in the rain. It meant trusting his father to meet his every need.

WHICH WAY
DO WE GO, DAD?

L. A. PARKER

FROM *FatherHEART*

A beautiful Northwest summer weekend found the Parker men sliding down glaciers, jumping streams and waking up marmots on a three-day father and son backpacking trip. It was a high time in the high country of Mt. Rainier National Park.

We had lingered on the mountain—it was all too good—but heading down the trail for home was now a destination trek. One of the greatest challenges on these trips—one that took me a while to learn—was to teach my sons to take their time on the trail. Look up, look around, there's so much more to see above your boots and the dusty trail. But like most guys, we were pretty destination oriented. We skipped and ran with our forty-pound packs most of the way down. Nate, in the lead and determined to win the race to the bottom, rounded a stretch of dense forest opening up to a fork in the trail. Not missing a stride, at breakneck speed, he turned his shoulder and shouted, "Which way do we go, Dad?" Shouting the answer back would have required more oxygen than I had in my heaving lungs so I simply stretched out my arm and pointed the way for him.

That simple question hit my heart like a train. My knees nearly buckled as I felt the rush and weight of the question lived out between fathers and sons over a lifetime. "Which way do we go, Dad?" That lucid picture of my responsibility and the honor of walking with my sons and showing them the way has never left me.

Our sons are calling on us to affirm their maleness, their gifts, who they are, what they do well—to show them the WAY!

FIRST DATE

NOLA BERTELSON

After more than forty years of marriage, my husband and I still enjoy sharing a chocolate malted milkshake on a date. We recently discovered an old-fashioned ice cream parlor pleasantly decorated in the style of the late 1930s. Their malts are topped with real whipped cream and served in tall frosty glasses on doily-lined glass plates.

As I took my first spoonful, my thoughts turned back to my very first date in an old-fashioned ice cream shop in Minnesota. A tall, handsome man, all spiffed-up, ushered a little brown-haired, seven-year-old girl into a high-back wooden booth. The little girl felt very special, proud and grown-up. She sat as tall as she could across the table from her handsome daddy. It was on this first date that he ordered my very first chocolate malted milkshake. Reminiscing now, it seems like a scene painted by Norman Rockwell on the cover of a *Saturday Evening Post*.

Isn't it wonderful how a certain atmosphere, or even a taste, can transport you back in time to relive pleasant memories?

THE LOVESICK
FATHER

PHILIP YANCEY

FROM *WHAT'S SO AMAZING ABOUT GRACE?*

A MODERN SETTING OF THE PARABLE IN LUKE 15:11–32

A young girl grows up on a cherry orchard just above Traverse City, Michigan. Her parents, a bit old-fashioned, tend to overreact to her nose ring, the music she listens to, and the length of her skirts. They ground her a few times, and she seethes inside. "I hate you!" she screams at her father when he knocks on the door of her room after an argument, and that night she acts on a plan she has mentally rehearsed scores of times. She runs away.

She had visited Detroit only once before, on a bus trip with her church youth group to watch the Tigers play. Because newspapers in Traverse City report in lurid detail the gangs, the drugs, and the violence in downtown Detroit, she concludes that this is probably the last place her parents will look for her. California, maybe, or Florida, but not Detroit.

Her second day there she meets a man who drives the biggest car she's ever seen. He offers her a ride, buys her lunch, arranges a place for her to stay. He gives her some pills that make her feel better than she's ever felt before. She was right all along, she decides: her parents were keeping her from all the fun.

The good life continues for a month, two months, a year. The man with the big car—she calls him "Boss"—teaches her a few things that men like. Since she's underage, men pay a premium for her. She lives in a penthouse, and orders room service whenever she wants. Occasionally she thinks about the folks back home, but their lives now seem so boring and provincial that she can hardly believe she grew up there.

She has a brief scare when she sees her picture printed on the back of a milk carton with the headline "Have you seen this child?" But by now she has blonde hair, and with all the makeup and body-piercing jewelry she wears, nobody would mistake her for a child. Besides, most of her friends are runaways, and nobody squeals in Detroit.

After a year the first sallow signs of illness appear, and it amazes her how fast the boss turns mean. "These days, we can't mess around," he growls, and before she knows it she's out on the street without a penny to her name. She still turns a couple of tricks a night, but they don't pay much, and all the money goes to support her habit. When winter blows in she finds herself sleeping on metal grates outside the big department stores. "Sleeping" is the wrong word—a teenage girl at night in downtown Detroit can never relax her guard. Dark bands circle her eyes. Her cough worsens.

One night as she lies awake listening for footsteps, all of a sudden everything about her life looks different. She no longer feels like a woman of the world. She feels like a little girl, lost in a cold and frightening city. She begins to whimper. Her pockets are empty and she's hungry. She needs a fix. She pulls her legs tight underneath her and shivers under the newspapers she's piled atop her coat. Something jolts a synapse of memory and a single image fills her mind: of May in Traverse City, when a million cherry trees bloom at once, with her golden retriever dashing through the rows and rows of blossomy trees in chase of a tennis ball.

God, why did I leave, she says to herself, and pain stabs at her heart. *My dog back home eats better than I do now.* She's sobbing, and she knows in a flash that more than anything else in the world she wants to go home.

Three straight phone calls, three straight connections with the answering machine. She hangs up without leaving a message the first two times, but the third time she says, "Dad, Mom, it's me. I was wondering about maybe coming home. I'm catching a bus up your way, and it'll get there about midnight tomorrow. If you're not there, well, I guess I'll just stay on the bus until it hits Canada."

It takes about seven hours for a bus to make all the stops between Detroit and Traverse City, and during that time she realizes the flaws in her plan. What if her parents are out of town and miss the message? Shouldn't she have waited another day or so until she could talk to them? And even if they are home, they probably wrote her off as dead long ago. She should have given them some time to overcome the shock.

Her thoughts bounce back and forth between those worries and the speech she is preparing for her father. "Dad, I'm sorry. I know I was wrong. It's not your fault; it's all mine. Dad, can you forgive me?" She says the words over and over, her throat tightening even as she rehearses them. She hasn't apologized to anyone in years.

The bus has been driving with lights on since Bay City. Tiny snowflakes hit the pavement rubbed worn by thousands of tires, and the asphalt steams. She's forgotten how dark it gets at night out here. A deer darts across the road and the bus swerves. Every so often, a billboard. A sign posting the mileage to Traverse City. *Oh, God.*

When the bus finally rolls into the station, its air brakes hissing in protest, the driver announces in a crackly voice over the microphone, "Fifteen minutes, folks. That's all we have here." Fifteen minutes to decide her life. She checks herself in a compact mirror, smoothes her hair, and licks the lipstick off her teeth. She looks at the tobacco stains on her fingertips, and wonders if her parents will notice. If they're here.

She walks into the terminal not knowing what to expect. Not one of the thousand scenes that have played out in her mind prepare her for what she sees. There, in the concrete-walls-and-plastic-chairs bus terminal in Traverse City, Michigan, stands a group of forty brothers and sisters and great-aunts and uncles and cousins and a grandmother and great-grandmother to boot. They're all wearing goofy party hats and blowing noise-makers, and taped across the entire wall of the terminal is a computer-generated banner that reads "Welcome home!"

Out of the crowd of well-wishers breaks her Dad. She stares out through the tears quivering in her eyes like hot mercury and begins the memorized speech, "Dad, I'm sorry. I know..."

He interrupts her. "Hush, child. We've got no time for that. No time for apologies. You'll be late for the party. A banquet's waiting for you at home."

MY UNBORN SON

WALTER S. SPARKS SR.

My son! What a simple, beautiful word!
    My boy! What a wonderful phrase!
We're counting the months, till you come to us—
    The months, and the weeks, and the days!

The new little stranger, some babies are called,
    But that's not what you're going to be,
With double my virtues, and half of my faults,
    You can't be a stranger to me.

Your mother is straight as a sapling plant,
    The cleanest and best of her clan—
You're bone of her bone, and flesh of her flesh,
    And by heaven we'll make you a man.

Soon I shall take you in two strong arms,
    You that shall howl for joy—
With a simple, passionate, wonderful pride,
    Because you are just—my boy.

And you shall lay in your mother's arms,
    And croon at your mother's breast,
And I shall thank God I am there to shield
    The two that I love the best.

A wonderful thing is a breaking wave,
    And sweet is the scent of spring,
But the silent voice of an unborn child
    Is God's most beautiful thing.

We're listening now to that silent voice
    And waiting, your mother and I—
Waiting to welcome the fruit of our love
    When you come to us, by and by.

We're hungry to show you a wonderful world
    With wonderful things to be done.
We're aching to give you the best of us both,
    We're lonely for you my son.

A HARD LESSON LEARNED

AARON RUPPERT

Time to get up," my dad said in a much too cheerful voice for 6 A.M.
I slowly climbed out of bed, not at all eager to face the full day's
work my dad had planned for me. With nearly one hundred head of cattle
and over a thousand acres of land, summer was always busy on the farm
and my dad made sure that I never ran out of things to do. He said that it
builds character for a sixteen-year-old boy to work hard, but all my friends
didn't have to work and I thought that they had plenty of character.

My job for the day was to mow one hundred acres of hay in three
fields, a mile from my house. The only good part about the job was that I
would be pulling my dad's new mower with the neighbor's car tractor we
borrowed, which had a radio and an air conditioner. The mower extended
nine feet out to the side of the tractor and could raise vertical to the
ground for transport on the road. After attaching the mower to the rear of
the tractor, I started out for the fields, taking time to get familiar with the
new equipment.

I began mowing around the outside of the field to allow more room
for turns. Then I divided the field into sections so I could make shorter
turns and work smaller areas. After I finished dividing up the field, I started
mowing the long rows. Hour after hour passed as I continued to mow

back and forth, raising the mower just slightly off the ground as I turned to head back for another pass. Nearing the end of the field, I put my hand on the hydraulic lever to raise the mower. As I emerged from the end of the field, I pulled back to raise the mower, but this time, instead of raising only an inch, the lever locked in the up position and the mower continued to rise.

Unaware that the mower was now high above the ground, I turned to go back for another pass. With the sharp turn and the mower now raised to vertical position, the tractor began to tip. Everything seemed to be happening in slow motion and yet I didn't have time to do anything. An instant later I was on my side in the overturned tractor. I immediately shut off the engine and climbed out of the door. I stood there on top of the overturned tractor for a while, disbelieving what had just happened. I climbed down and began walking back to the house, looking back periodically to make sure the tractor was still on its side and I wasn't imagining things. My thoughts soon turned to a much more important dilemma: how was I going to tell my dad that I wrecked the eight-thousand-dollar mower and the neighbor's sixty-thousand-dollar tractor in less than a second?

I finally reached the house, but Dad was gone so I went inside to wait. After the longest forty-five minutes of my life, dad drove into the driveway and I went out to meet him. He could tell that something was wrong by the look on my face. When he asked me what had happened, it took all the strength I had to tell him without bursting into tears.

"Let's go see what she looks like," was all he said as he walked over to the truck. Finally, I began to cry. Dad gave me a reassuring look and told me everything would be okay. I wasn't quite ready to believe him, but he soon proved to be right. We pulled the tractor back onto its wheels. To our surprise, there was little damage.

For a while, my story was big news at all the area coffee shops, but at the time I had no idea of the effect that incident would have on me. As I look back, I see a change from a sixteen-year-old boy to a sixteen-year-old man. Not only was my dad giving me work to do, but he was giving me responsibility as well. He was teaching me to be accountable for my actions, and to fix the mistakes I made. My dad could have treated me like the immature boy that I was, but instead he treated me like a man. I began to see what he meant when he talked about character. Character is not automatically acquired at a certain age. It is something that is taught over time by those we love and respect. I have a lot more to learn about life, but it's comforting to know that whatever I go through, I not only have a father who will always be there for me, I also have a friend.

BUILD ME A SON

O, Lord…
Build me a son whose heart will be clear,
whose goal will be high,
a son who will master himself
before he seeks to master other men;
one who will reach into the future,
yet never forget the past.

GENERAL DOUGLAS MACARTHUR

THE BALE OF BINDER TWINE

CHARLIE SHEDD

FROM *YOU CAN BE A GREAT PARENT*

I promise you that I will never say "No" if I can possibly say "Yes." We see it often. Babies raised in a positive atmosphere develop much better personalities than those who constantly hear the words "No," "Stop," "Don't."

Let me show you what I mean. This has to do with a dirty old bale of binder twine. When we moved from Nebraska to Oklahoma, we brought it along. I had used it there to tie sacks of feed and miscellaneous items. It cost something like $1.15. So I said, "Now, Philip, you see this binder twine? I want you to leave it alone." But it held a strange fascination for him and he began to use it any time he wanted. I would say, "Don't," "No," and "You can't!" But all to no avail.

That went on for six or eight months. Then one day I came home, tired. There was the garage, looking like a no-man's land with binder twine across, back and forth, up and down. And was I provoked! I ground my teeth as I slashed at that binder twine. Suddenly, when I was halfway through the maze, a light dawned. I asked myself, "Why do you want this binder twine? What if Philip does use it?" So when I went in to supper that night, Philip was there and I began, "Say, about that binder twine!" He hung his head, and mumbled, "Yes, Daddy." Then I said, "Philip, I've changed my mind. You can use that old binder twine any time you want. What's more, all those tools out in the garage I've labeled 'No'—you go ahead and use them. I can buy new tools, but I can't buy new boys." There never was a sunrise like that smile. "Thanks, Daddy," he beamed. And guess what? He hasn't touched that binder twine since!

LONGING

You have just finished a run, and you are sitting on the porch sweating like a horse and smelling like one, and your son, or perhaps a little neighbor boy, sits down next to you, leans against you, and says, "You smell good." This is the primal longing for one's father.

KENT HUGHES

FROM *DISCIPLINES OF A GODLY MAN*

THE POWER OF A PICTURE

JOHN TRENT

FROM *CHOOSING TO LIVE THE BLESSING*

Movies affect us not only culturally but personally. The images flashed on movie screens are images we take with us when we leave the theater. They have a subliminal effect on us that is enormous. The images shape our understanding of how we should relate husband to wife, parent to child, friend to friend.

Take this image for example.

Marion doesn't seem a very manly name, but it was the name of the movie star who became an icon of manliness for millions. His full name was Marion Michael Morrison. His film name was John Wayne. The Duke.

The images he left behind on the screen impacted the male consciousness for over four decades. His pictures projected the image of a man who was his own man, a man nobody owned or ordered around. He pulled himself up by his bootstraps. He shot straight and rode tall. He went *his* way, on his own horse. And he was famous for lines like the one he delivered in the film *She Wore a Yellow Ribbon:* "Never apologize, mister. It's a sign of weakness."

It's not true, of course. But hearing the Duke say it and seeing him on the screen larger than life, it seems it should be true.

That is the power of a picture, especially the picture of someone we look up to. Even if what he or she says isn't true, it seems true to us because the person looms larger than life. That person may be a movie star, a coach, a teacher.

Or a father.

The following thoughts are from a man reflecting on the pictures he had left one day in his son's life. I think he's the type of man John Wayne would have wanted as a father...before he was the Duke and was just little Marion.

Listen, son, I am saying this as you lie asleep, one little paw crumpled under your cheek and the blonde curls sticky wet on your forehead. Just a few moments ago, I sat, reading my paper in the library, and a stifling wave of remorse swept over me. Guiltily I came to your bedside.

These are the things I was thinking, son: I had been cross to you. I scolded you as you were crossing the street because you didn't look both ways before coming over to see me; I didn't like it, and told you so when you just gave your face a dab with the towel. I took you to task for not cleaning your shoes. I called angrily when you threw some of your things on the floor.

At breakfast I found fault, too. You spilled things. You gulped down your food. You put your elbows on the table. You spread butter too thick on your bread. And as you started off to play, and I made for my bus, you turned and waved a hand and called, "Goodbye, Daddy," and I frowned and said in reply, "Hold your shoulders back."

Then it began all over again in the late afternoon. As I came up the road I spied you, down on your knees, playing marbles. There were holes in your stockings. I humiliated you before your boy friends by marching you straight to the house ahead of me. Stockings were expensive—and if you had to buy them, you'd be more careful....

Do you remember later, when I was reading in the library, how you came in timidly, with a sort of hurt look in your eyes? When I glanced up over my paper, impatient at the interruption, you hesitated at the door, and I snapped, "What do you want?"

You said nothing, just ran across in one tempestuous plunge, threw your arms around my neck and kissed me. And then you were gone, pattering up the stairs.

Well, son, it was shortly afterward that my paper slipped from my hands and a terrible sickening feeling came over me. What has habit been doing to me? The habit of finding fault, or reprimanding.... It was not that I didn't love you; it was that I expected too much of you. I was measuring you by the yardstick of my own years.

There's so much that is good and fine in your little character. It didn't matter what I said, you came in with a spontaneous burst of childish emotion, and rushed across the room to kiss me goodnight. Nothing else matters tonight, son. I have come to your bedside in the darkness, and I have knelt there, ashamed!...

Tomorrow, son, I'll be a real daddy. I'll be kind and thoughtful. I'll laugh when you laugh, and cry when you cry. Don't worry about me, son. I'll remember how important you are, and I'll remember who you are.

I'm afraid I've visualized you as a man. Yet, as I look at you now, son, peacefully sleeping in your little bed, I see that you are still a baby. Yesterday you were in your mother's arms, your head on her shoulder. I have asked too much.

I have expected you to be a man, son, and you're only a little boy.

My little boy.

W. Livingston Larned
from "A Father Forgets"

As you look at your little boy or girl—at your older brother or younger sister, at your arthritic mother or aging father, at your pastor or youth worker or school administrator or best friend—don't be afraid to apologize. Don't just rehearse it in your mind or confess it in your prayers by the bedside of the one you've hurt. Pick the right time to talk about it, but talk about it.

No matter what anybody tells you, apologizing isn't a sign of weakness.

It's a sign of strength.

*If you take being a father seriously, you'll know that you're
not big enough for the job, not by yourself.... Being a father
will put you on your knees if nothing else ever did.*

ELISABETH ELLIOT

FROM *THE MARK OF A MAN*

MIKE AND THE GRASS

ERMA BOMBECK

FROM *FOREVER, ERMA*

When Mike was three, he wanted a sandbox, and his father said, "There goes the yard. We'll have kids over here day and night, and they'll throw sand into the flower beds, and cats will make a mess in it, and it'll kill the grass for sure."

And Mike's mother said, "It'll come back."

When Mike was five, he wanted a jungle-gym set with swings that would take his breath away and bars to take him to the summit, and his father said, "Good grief, I've seen those things in backyards, and do you know what they look like? Mud holes in a pasture. Kids digging their gym shoes in the ground. It'll kill the grass."

And Mike's mother said, "It'll come back."

Between breaths when Daddy was blowing up the plastic swimming pool, he warned, "You know what they're going to do to this place? They're going to condemn it and use it for a missile site. I hope you know what you're doing. They'll track water everywhere and have a million water fights, and you won't be able to take out the garbage without stepping in mud up to your neck. When we take this down, we'll have the only brown lawn on the block."

"It'll come back," Mike's mother said.

When Mike was 12, he volunteered his yard for a camp-out. As they hoisted the tents and drove in the spikes, his father stood at the window and observed: "Why don't I just put the grass seed out in cereal bowls for the birds and save myself trouble spreading it around? You know for a fact that those tents and all those big feet are going to trample down every single blade of grass, don't you? Don't bother to answer. I know what you're going to say. 'It'll come back.'"

The basketball hoop on the side of the garage attracted more crowds than the Olympics. And a small patch of lawn that started out with a barren spot the size of a garbage can lid soon grew to encompass the entire side yard.

Just when it looked as if the new seed might take root, the winter came and the sled runners beat it into ridges. Mike's father shook his head and said, "I never asked for much in this life—only a patch of grass."

And his wife smiled and said, "It'll come back."

The lawn this fall was beautiful. It was green and alive and rolled out like a sponge carpet along the drive where gym shoes had trod…along the garage where bicycles used to fall…and around the flower beds where little boys used to dig with iced-tea spoons.

But Mike's father never saw it. He anxiously looked beyond the yard and asked with a catch in his voice, "He will come back, won't he?"

OUR GIRL

MAX LUCADO

FROM *SIX HOURS ONE FRIDAY*

Jenna, wake up. It's time to go to school."

She will hear those words a thousand times in her life. But she heard them for the first time this morning.

I sat on the edge of her bed for a while before I said them to her. To tell the truth, I didn't want to say them. I didn't want to wake her. A queer hesitancy hung over me as I sat in the early morning blackness. As I sat in silence, I realized that my words would awaken her to a new world.

For four lightning-fast years she'd been ours, and ours alone. And now that was all going to change.

We put her to bed last night as "our girl"—exclusive property of Mommy and Daddy. Mommy and Daddy read to her, taught her, listened to her. But beginning today, someone else would, too.

Until today, it was Mommy and Daddy who wiped away the tears and put on the Band-Aids. But beginning today, someone else would, too.

I didn't want to wake her.

Until today, her life was essentially us—Mom, Dad, and baby sister Andrea. Today that life would grow—new friends, a teacher. Her world was this house—her room, her toys, her swing set. Today her world would expand. She would enter the winding halls of education—painting, reading, calculating…becoming.

I didn't want to wake her. Not because of the school. It's a fine one. Not because I don't want her to learn. Heaven knows I want her to grow, to read, to mature. Not because she doesn't want to go. School has been all she could talk about for the last week!

No, I didn't want to wake her up because I didn't want to give her up.

But I woke her anyway. I interrupted her childhood with the inevitable proclamation, "Jenna, wake up…it's time to go to school."

It took me forever to get dressed. Denalyn saw me moping around and heard me humming, "Sunrise, Sunset" and said, "You'll never make it through her wedding." She's right.

We took her to school in two cars so that I could go directly to work. I asked Jenna to ride with me. I thought I should give her a bit of fatherly assurance. As it turned out, I was the one needing assurance.

For one dedicated to the craft of words, I found very few to share with her. I told her to enjoy herself. I told her to obey her teacher. I told her, "If you get lonely or afraid, tell your teacher to call me and I'll come and get you." "Okay," she smiled. Then she asked if she could listen to a tape with kids' music. "Okay," I said.

So while she sang songs, I swallowed lumps. I watched her as she sang. She looked big. Her little neck stretched as high as it could to look over the dash. Her eyes were hungry and bright. Her hands were folded in her lap. Her feet, wearing brand new turquoise and pink tennis shoes, barely extended over the seat….

Sunrise, sunset; sunrise, sunset;
Swiftly fly the days.[1]

"Denalyn was right," I mumbled to myself. "I'll never make it through the wedding."

What is she thinking? I wondered. *Does she know how tall this ladder of education is that she will begin climbing this morning?*

No, she didn't. But I did. How many chalkboards will those eyes see? How many books will those hands hold? How many teachers will those feet follow and—gulp—imitate?

Were it within my power, I would have, at that very instant, assembled all the hundreds of teachers, instructors, coaches, and tutors that she would have over the next eighteen years and announced, "This is no normal student. This is my child. Be careful with her!"

As I parked and turned off the engine, my big girl became small again. But it was a voice of a very little girl that broke the silence. "Daddy, I don't want to get out."

I looked at her. The eyes that had been bright were now fearful. The lips that had been singing were now trembling.

I fought a Herculean urge to grant her request. Everything within me wanted to say, "Okay, let's forget it and get out of here." For a brief, eternal moment I considered kidnapping my own daughters, grabbing my wife, and escaping these horrid paws of progress to live forever in the Himalayas.

But I knew better. I knew it was time. I knew it was right. And I knew she would be fine. But I never knew it would be so hard to say, "Honey, you'll be all right. Come on, I'll carry you."

And she *was* all right. One step into the classroom and the cat of curiosity pounced on her. And I walked away. I gave her up. Not much. And not as much as I will have to in the future. But I gave her up as much as I could today.

1. "Sunrise, Sunset" (Jerry Bock, Sheldon Harnick), © 1964—Alley Music Corp. and Trio Music Co., Inc.

SPORTS

MY HERO

During the winter of 1993, workers at the Baseball Hall of Fame in Cooperstown, Ohio, made a remarkable, heartwarming discovery. While renovating a section of the museum, they found a photograph that had been hidden in a crevice underneath a display case. The man in the picture has a bat resting on his shoulders; he's wearing a uniform with the words "Sinclair Oil" printed across his chest; his demeanor is gentle and friendly. Stapled to the picture is a note, scribbled in pen by an adoring fan. The note reads:

> *You were never too tired to play ball. On your days off, you helped build the Little League Field. You always came to watch me play. You were a Hall of Fame Dad. I wish I could share this moment with you.* Your Son, Peter

> *A son named Pete found a creative way to put his dad in the Hall of Fame.*

ROBERT LEWIS

FROM *REAL FAMILY VALUES*

THEY WANT ME
FOR ONE REASON

DAVID DRAVECKY

FROM *WHEN YOU CAN'T COME BACK*

E ver since that backyard game of catch with my dad, baseball had become my life. It's what I watched on TV when I was indoors. It's what I played when I went outdoors. It's what I read about when I sprawled on the living room floor and spread out the Sunday paper.

My life was wrapped up in baseball. And my life as a ballplayer was wrapped up in my arm. It wasn't long before that arm gained the attention of the neighborhood. When they chose up sides for sandlot ball, I was the one they all wanted on their team.

They wanted me for one reason—my arm.

It wasn't long before that arm caught the attention of the entire school, when, as a teenager, I pitched my first no-hitter. My name started showing up on the sports page. Before long it made the headlines.

All because of my arm.

That arm attracted the attention of major league scouts, and the part of me that was my boyhood became my livelihood. My ability to provide for my family was not based on how good of a personality I had, how smart I was, or how hard I worked. It was based solely on what my arm could do on game day. The more strikes that arm could throw, the more I was worth. The more games that arm won, the more people wanted me on their team.

When people talked with me, it was the center of conversation. "How's the arm today, Dave?" "Is your arm ready for tonight?" "Better get some ice on that arm; don't want it to swell."

My arm was to me what hands are to a concert pianist, what legs are to a ballerina, what feet are to a marathon runner. It's what people cheered me for, what they paid their hard-earned money to see. It's what made me valuable, what gave me worth, at least in the eyes of the world.

Then suddenly my arm was gone.

How much of me went with it? How much of what people thought of me went with it?

I felt apprehensive. I wondered how my son would react when he saw me. Would he be afraid? Would he feel sorry for me? Would he keep his distance? And what about my daughter? Would she be embarrassed when we went out to eat? How would she feel when people stared? How would my wife feel? What would she think about a man who couldn't tie his own shoes? Would she still find me attractive, or would she be repulsed to see me in my nakedness with my carved-up body?

When I came home from the hospital, I realized that all Jonathan wanted was to wrestle with me and play football on the lawn. All Tiffany wanted was to hug me. All Jan wanted was to have her husband back.

They didn't care whether I had an arm or not.

As important as it had been to my boyhood, as important as it had been to my livelihood, my arm meant nothing to the people in my life who mattered the most. It was enough that I was alive and that I was home.

A LESSON FROM THE MOUND

BETH MULLALLY

FROM *TIMES HERALD-RECORD*

My father was always the pitcher in our back-yard baseball games. He got this honor in part because my sister, brother and I couldn't get the ball over home plate, but also because, with one wooden leg, running after a fly ball that got hit into the cornfield out back just wasn't his strong suit. And so he'd stand under the hot sun, pitching endlessly while we took turns at bat.

He ran our games with the authority of a Yankees manager. He was boss, and he had requirements. We had to chatter in the outfield, for one. I must have said "Nobatternobatternobatternobatter" 5000 times while growing up. And we had to try to outrun the ball, no matter how futile it might seem. This was baseball, by golly, and there was only one way to play: the way the Yankees played.

Going up to bat against my father was not easy. None of this self-esteem stuff for him, trying to make a kid feel good about hitting a ball that's standing still. He was never the least bit sorry when he struck me out, and he did it all the time. "Do you want to play ball or don't you?" he'd ask if I began whining about his fast pitches.

I wanted to. And when I'd finally connect with the ball—oh, man, I knew I deserved the hit. I'd be grinning all the way down the first-base line.

I'd turn to look at my father on the pitcher's mound. He'd take off his glove and tuck it under his arm, and then clap for me. To my ears, it sounded like a standing ovation at Yankee stadium.

Years later, my son was to learn those same rules about baseball from my father. By then, though, Dad was pitching from a wheelchair. In some medical fluke, he had lost his other leg.

But nothing else had changed. My boy was required to chatter from the outfield. He had to try outrunning the ball, no matter how futile it might seem. And when he whined that the pitch was too fast, he got the ultimatum: "Do you want to play ball or don't you?"

He did.

My boy was nine years old the spring before his grandfather died. They played a lot of ball that season, and there was the usual litany of complaints that my father was pitching too hard.

"Just keep your eye on the ball!" Dad would holler at him.

Finally, at one at-bat, he did. He swung and connected dead-center. The ball slammed down the middle, straight at my father.

He reached for it, but missed. And in the process, his wheelchair tilted backward. In ever such slow motion, we watched him and his chair topple until he came down on his back with a thud.

My boy stood stock-still halfway to first.

"You don't ever stop running!" my father roared from the ground. "That ball's still in play! You run!"

When my boy stood safe at first base, he turned to look at my father lying on his back on the pitcher's mound. He saw him take off his glove and tuck it under his arm. And then he heard his grandfather clap for him.

(Reprinted with permission from the April 1994 *Reader's Digest*.)

BARCELONA OLYMPICS 1992

IVAN MAISEL

FROM *THE DALLAS MORNING NEWS, AUGUST 4, 1992*

BARCELONA, SPAIN—Jim Redmond did what any father would do. His child needed help. It was that simple. The Olympic Games have the kind of security that thousands of policemen and metal detectors can offer. But no venue is safe when a father sees his son's dream drifting away.

"One minute I was running," Derek Redmond of Great Britain said. "The next thing was a pop. I went down."

Derek, 26, had waited for this 400-meter semifinal for at least four years. In Seoul, he had an Achilles tendon problem. He waited until a minute-and-a-half before the race began before he would admit he couldn't run.

In November 1990, Derek underwent operations on both Achilles tendons. He has had five surgeries in all. But he came back. In the first two rounds he had run 45.02 and 45.03, his fastest times in five years.

"I really wanted to compete in my first Olympics," Redmond said. "I was feeling great. It just came out of the blue."

Halfway around the track, Redmond lay sprawled across lane 5, his right hamstring gone bad.

Redmond struggled to his feet and began hobbling around the track.

The winner of the heat, defending Olympic champion Steve Lewis, had finished and headed toward the tunnel. So had the other six runners. But the last runner in the heat hadn't finished. He continued to run.

Jim Redmond (Derek's dad), sitting high in the stands at Olympic Stadium, saw Derek collapse.

"You don't need accreditation in an emergency," Redmond said.

So Redmond, a 49-year-old machine shop owner in Northampton, ran down the steps and onto the track.

"I was thinking," Jim Redmond said, "I had to get him there so he could say he finished the semifinal."

The crowd realized that Derek Redmond was running the race of his life. Around the stands, from around the world, the fans stood and honored him with cheers.

At the final turn, Jim Redmond caught up to his son and put his arm around him. Derek leaned on his dad's right shoulder and sobbed. But they kept going. An usher attempted to intercede and escort Jim Redmond off the track. If ever a futile mission had been undertaken....

They crossed the finish line, father and son, arm in arm.

Many men go fishing their entire lives
without knowing it is not fish they are after.

HENRY DAVID THOREAU

THE VIKING COWBOY

RUTH SENTER

FROM *STARTLED BY SILENCE*

W hen does a job become more important than the people you love?" I've often asked myself that question. In an unexpected way, I met my answer.

His ten-gallon hat barely cleared the doorway as he boarded Flight 721 in St. Louis. As he moved his towering frame down the aisle, swung his genuine cowhide case into the overhead compartment, and eased into the seat next to mine, I could tell this was no ordinary cowboy.

He was as cool and masculine as any aftershave commercial. He knew all the right lines and used them generously on everyone around him. I buried myself in my *Mainliner* magazine and tried not to notice. I wasn't enamored with a cowboy who appeared to have an ego twice the size of his hat. And I wasn't about to fall for his act.

"That a good article?" his voice boomed in my direction.

"Uh-huh."

"Ever heard of the Minnesota Vikings? I play football for them."

Something in his tone sounded haunting. I sensed there was more he wanted to say. I closed my magazine and listened. He glanced across the aisle, then back at me. No one was watching. He quit acting.

"Golden boy. Down the tubes." As he motioned thumbs down, I

noticed his ring with an NFL insignia.

"See these eyes? They're red from crying. Just left my wife and two sons. Can't even be with them anymore. Kicked out of my own house. Didn't know football players cried, did you?"

As the 727 roared toward Chicago, he spilled out the pieces of his broken dream. Hard work. Irregular schedules. Frequent moves. Always the excuse that someday they would have time for each other. But one day there was no more someday.

"You know what my job became?" he asked. "An ego trip, that's what! After a while, my job was everything. Couldn't even hear what my family was saying.

"You write articles. Tell your readers that when a job makes you deaf to your family, you'd better *quit*. Tell 'em I said so—and I ought to know!"

We pulled up to the United gate, but even the congestion on Concourse E didn't interrupt the cowboy's discourse. "You've got your family," he exclaimed. "Hang on to them for all you're worth. Make them feel they're the most important thing to you. It's an empty world without them. I ought to know."

He tipped his ten-gallon hat in my direction, and I watched him climb into his waiting limousine and head for downtown Chicago. *Tomorrow,* I thought, *he'll be back running touchdowns.*

"Tell your readers," he'd said to me, "when your job makes you deaf to your family, you'd better quit." I promised him I would.

THE BEST
CHRISTMAS

AUTHOR UNKNOWN

FROM *REVELL'S BOOK OF ILLUSTRATIONS*

There was an old fellow living on Skid Row, completely down and out and living on what he could beg, borrow or steal along the Row. One Christmas Eve he found a dollar bill; it was a fortune to such a man, and he thought long of what he ought to do with it. Finally he decided to treat his fellow tramps along the waterfront to an extra drink to celebrate this holiday, and he started for the waterfront.

Along his route he saw a baseball bat in the window of a sports shop; the haunting memory of how much he had wanted a bat like that when he was a boy burned in his heart like fire, and he rushed into the shop, bought the bat with his dollar bill, went down the street and left it propped up against the door of an orphanage. He rang the bell and ran. The bat was given that Christmas to a homely, awkward little orphan who loved to play ball, but up to that time never had a bat of his own. It was his best Christmas.... You may know him by the name he had when he became home run king in the big leagues; it was Babe Ruth.

It was probably the vagrant's best Christmas, too....

BENCHED

JAMES ROBISON

FROM *MY FATHER'S FACE*

I remember an occasion when our son Randy played extremely well in Little League baseball. He had actually batted .500 that year and, as I recall, had only two singles. He was primarily hitting doubles—and also some triples and home runs. He was consistently driving the ball up against the outfield fence on one or two bounces—good enough for extra bases in Little League. He was having the year of his life, and this daddy felt pretty puffed up about it all....

Yet even with the great year he was having, Randy seemed to be on the bench quite a bit as the coaches tried to play as many boys as possible. Always polite, Randy had a great attitude about it, and seemed content to give others their turn in the spotlight. He wasn't struggling a bit.

But I was!

More than once, I told that coach how I felt about it. How could he pull a kid who was having such a year? How could he replace him with boys who didn't care nearly as much or play nearly as well? Didn't he want to win? Wasn't he sending the wrong signals by benching the kids who were playing the hardest and best?

As a matter of fact, there really were some wrong signals on that field. But they weren't coming from the coach. It was my own impatient, win-at-all-costs attitude that was sending the wrong signals!

Randy didn't like having his dad in the coach's face. It made him nervous and embarrassed him. He would find himself looking over his shoulder, wondering how Dad was going to react to this or that decision. It was something of a shadow right in the midst of that superb year. Down in my heart, I knew that my attitude bothered him—and I asked the Lord to help me back off a little.

When Randy made the all-star team we were all excited as could be. I can remember flying home and getting to one of the all-star games just a little bit late. As I walked up to the ball diamond from the parking lot, I could see that Randy's team was already in the field and my heart started pounding a little bit harder.

But where was Randy? I approached the bleachers and there he was, sitting by himself on the bench. Good night! It didn't make sense! This was the kid who led the league in batting averages and had played so well in the field. And he was starting the all-star game *on the bench?*

Randy looked unsmilingly over his shoulder as he watched me take my seat in the bleachers. Seeing the expression on his face, I honestly felt as though I could read his mind. He was thinking: *Oh, man. I know Dad is really disappointed and upset to see me on the bench. Dear God, please don't let him say anything or let it show.*

By the grace of God, that was one of those moments when I finally got it right. While I was still in my car driving from the airport to the game, I felt strongly impressed that I somehow needed to convey to that young man how thoroughly proud I was of him—and that he didn't need to "perform" to get my approval.

I walked over to the fence and leaned over. My boy looked up, somewhat apprehensively.

"Randy," I said, "I want you to know Dad is just as proud of you sitting right here on this bench as I would be if you were starting third base and hitting home runs. There's no way I could ever be more proud of you. You're my son, and you don't have to do anything to please me or to gain my approval. You've got it a hundred percent. I love you, son."

Tears filled his eyes and he smiled. Somehow I knew I had touched a chord. And with thanks in my heart to God, I knew I had done exactly the right thing.

Progress always involves risk;
you can't steal second base and keep your foot on first.
ANONYMOUS

HE'S YOUR FISH, SON

MARTY TRAMMELL

The swells of the Straits of Juan de Fuca seemed to toy with Dad's 14-foot Lund as we searched for Kings in front of what locals called "the cave" near Sekiu, Washington. "This isn't all that bad," I thought as I reached into Dad's green tackle box for another peanut-butter cracker. The sloshing in my ten-year-old belly was finally giving way to the crackers and the excitement brought on by the brightening yellow glow in the east.

"Make sure you hold your mouth right, son. The bite's comin'." Dad put his coffee cup back into the holder he had bolted to the wood seat that summer.

I studied his mouth, looking for the secret grownups never reveal to each other but pass down to their sons like the Old Timer knife Dad gave me for my tenth birthday. Although I couldn't tell exactly how Dad was holding his mouth, I was convinced this was the secret to Dad's success with salmon.

I stuck my tongue in the corner of my cheek and waited, staring at the eye staring back at me on the end of my 6-foot salmon rod. Suddenly, my face felt hot and the boat seemed to exaggerate its motion with every swell. Up, down, up, down. The green and white pole in my hand became two poles, then three. Dad eyed my changing appearance cautiously.

"Oh, oh, looks like it's time to feed the fish," Dad's voice sounded muffled, so far away.

"Feed the fish?" I puzzled, looking down at the frozen herring in the package at my feet. That was all it took. Seconds later, pieces of cracker and peanut butter floated behind the eighteen-horse Johnson.

"You'll feel better when it quits hurtin'," Dad assured, his cheeks vibrating with the throttle in his left hand. Before I could even think through the significance of Dad's comment, something tried to rip the fiberglass pole out of my frozen fingers.

"Fish on!" Dad's yell echoed from the boat to the shore and back.

"What do I do?" I pleaded.

"Just keep your tip up and don't stop reeling."

I reeled as fast as I could while Dad swung the Lund around in the direction of my rapidly descending line.

"I can't do it, Dad. It's too strong." My arms ached after only seconds of trying to hold the tip of the pole above my head. Exhausted, I succumbed and the rod crashed against the edge of the oar lock.

"Keep your tip up, son, you don't want to lose him." Dad's face was bright and glowing.

"I can't, Dad. My arms hurt. You reel for me!" My forearms and wrists begged with me, as the salmon continued to dive.

"He's your fish, son."

"But I can't keep my tip up, Dad. I can't reel. You gotta help me."

"You can do it. Put your leg over the end of the rod. It'll help you keep your tip out of the water." I saw my dad reach for the pole and then quickly pull his hand away. "He's your fish, son. We're gonna get him. You wait and see."

Somewhere from deep inside me new strength surfaced, and fifteen minutes later, so did the 20-pound King.

"There he is!" Dad let go of the throttle and grabbed for the net. The little Lund rocked sideways, slamming my knees into the aluminum rivets that held the boat together. Dad grabbed the belt loop on my Levis and yanked me back into my seat. I stuck the end of the pole under my leg again and repeated the circular reeling motion.

One turn. The muscle-rending strain of the fish made the small distance my wrist had to turn seem like a mile.

Two turns. The line edged one inch, two inches—dragging the salmon closer.

Three turns. I felt the fish give up.

"Hold on, son, just a few more minutes." Dad seemed to talk more to the fish than to me.

"A few more minutes?" I thought. "Isn't he going to net the fish?" My questions were drowned by the singing of my reel, as the salmon powered his way downward, rubbing his victory in my face with each yard of line he tore from my spool.

"Not again!" I sobbed. "I'll never get him!" The aches doubled instantly. I was beat.

"Dad, I'm gonna lose him. You've gotta reel him in! Please, Dad." I tried to move my wrists around and around, but the salmon's dive was stronger. The leg I had put over the end of the pole lifted off the wood seat, and I slid toward the ocean. Dad grabbed for me again and pulled me back.

"You almost have him now. He's your fish, son. Don't give up." I saw him reach for the pole again. This time his hand moved back more slowly. I searched for strength within, but nothing came.

I prayed, "Please God, just this one fish. I promise I'll go to church for the rest of my life and be nice to my sister." I felt sure God liked fishing since he'd given Jonah quite a story. I wasn't sure what he thought about my sister.

Suddenly, the line went limp. It was the most horrible feeling I had ever felt. The fish was gone. All that work. All that aching. For what?

"Son, keep reeling! He's comin' straight toward the boat!" Dad's voice shattered my sobs, and I reeled faster than I knew possible. The empty spool began to fill with line. Dad grabbed the net with one hand, scooted me to the opposite side of the boat with the other, and lunged toward the line. His knees slammed against the aluminum frame as he buried his arms and the net beneath the boat.

For what seemed longer than a math class, Dad stayed there. Bent over. Silent. Then with a sudden surge, his shoulders shot backward, his back straightened, and the net and the biggest fish I'd ever seen came flying straight over Dad's head into the boat.

That was the first and only time I stood up in that 14-foot Lund.

Neighboring fishermen cheered as I held the fish up, my fingers through his right gills and I am sure, now, my Dad's through his left. I looked up into Dad's face and saw the widest smile and the first tears I had ever seen.

It proved the biggest salmon on Olson's dock that day. At least, it was the biggest one I saw. All the way back to Tretevick's campground, I stared back through the window of Dad's 1970 Chevy at the long silver body draped across a dull-red fish box. The pain in my arms and back, although numbed by the sight of the salmon, reminded me what I had done. I had reeled in a fish when all my strength was gone. I had done something I felt I couldn't do. And now, the best fish I had ever seen had my name written all over him.

My family gathered around for the picture. Mom focused the camera and counted "One, two…" As a smile stretched over my face and I struggled to keep the fish's tail out of the dirt, my dad put his arm on my shoulder, and I heard him whisper again:

"He's your fish, son!"

NOTHING TO PROVE

KENNETH BOA

FROM *THAT I MAY KNOW GOD*

J oe Louis was the world heavyweight boxing champion from 1937 until he retired in 1949. During his time of service in the army, Louis was driving with a fellow GI when he was involved in a minor collision with a large truck. The truck driver got out, yelling and swearing at Louis, who just sat in the driver's seat, smiling. "Why didn't you get out and knock him flat?" asked his buddy after the truck driver had moved on. "Why should I?" replied Joe. "When somebody insulted Caruso, did he sing an aria for him?"

This is one of my favorite illustrations because it is so relevant to the theme of identity. The truck driver clearly didn't know the real identity of the person he was cursing, for if he had, he would have treated him in a dramatically different way! On the other hand, Joe Louis knew who he was—the best boxer in the world—and therefore he had nothing to prove.

THE WINNER

SHARON JAYNES

I t was the first swim meet of the year for our newly formed Middle School Aquatics team. The atmosphere on the three hour bus ride was electric with anticipation as the band of forty-eight adolescents thought of nothing but victory. However, the electricity turned into shock as our minnows filed off the bus and stared in disbelief at their muscle clad Greek-god-like opponents.

The coach checked the schedule. "Surely there's been a mistake," he thought. But the schedule only confirmed that, yes, this was the right place and the right time.

The two teams formed a line on the side of the pool. Whistles blew, races were begun, and races were lost. Halfway through the meet, Coach Huey realized that he had no participants for one of the events.

"OK team, who wants to swim the 500 yard free style?" the coach asked.

Several hands shot up, including Justin Rigsbee's. "I'll race, Coach!"

The coach looked down at the freckle faced youth and said, "Justin, this race is twenty lengths of the pool. I've only seen you swim eight."

"Oh, I can do it, Coach. Let me try. What's twelve more laps?"

Coach Huey reluctantly conceded. "After all," he thought, "it's not the winning but the trying that builds character."

The whistle blew and the opponents torpedoed through the water and finished the race in a mere four minutes and fifty seconds. The winners gathered on the sidelines to socialize while our group struggled to finish. After four more long minutes, the last exhausted members of our team emerged from the water. The last except for Justin.

Justin was stealing breaths as his hands slapped against the water and pushed it aside to propel his thin body forward. It appeared that he would go under at any minute, yet something seemed to keep pushing him onward.

"Why doesn't the coach stop this child?" the parents whispered among themselves. "He looks like he's about to drown and the race was won four minutes ago."

But what the parents did not realize was that the real race, the race of a boy becoming a man, was just beginning.

The coach walked over to the young swimmer, knelt down and quietly spoke.

Relieved parents thought, *Oh, he's finally going to pull that boy out before he kills himself.*

But to their surprise, the coach rose from the concrete, stepped back from the pool's edge, and the young man continued to swim.

One teammate, inspired by his brave friend, went to the side of the pool and walked the lane as Justin pressed on. "Come on, Justin, you can do it! You can do it! Keep going! Don't give up!"

He was joined by another, then another, until the entire team was walking the length of the pool rooting for and encouraging their fellow swimmer to finish the race set before him.

The opposing team saw what was happening and joined the chant. The students' contagious chorus sent a chill through the room and soon the once concerned parents were on their feet cheering, shouting, and praying. The room was pulsating with energy and excitement as teammates and opponents alike pumped courage into one small swimmer.

Twelve long minutes after the starting whistle had blown, an exhausted, but smiling, Justin Rigsbee swam his final lap and pulled himself out of the pool. The crowd had applauded the first swimmer as he crossed the line in first place. But the standing ovation they gave Justin that day was proof that the greater victory was his, just for finishing the race.

A CHANCE TO PLAY BASEBALL

Ernie Banks, the Chicago Cubs Hall of Fame baseball player, always remembered the way his father worked and sacrificed to give him the chance to play baseball. Everyday his father left the house before dawn and got home after dark. He worked so many hours that he hardly ever saw sunlight. When Ernie signed his first contract with the Cubs, he sent a three-word telegram to his dad. "We did it!"

AUTHOR UNKNOWN

FROM MORE OF...THE BEST OF BITS & PIECES

UNEXPECTED PLACES

ROCHELLE M. PENNINGTON

I t has been my experience that one stumbles across life's most profound lessons in the most unexpected places—places like a neighborhood Little League baseball diamond.

Our sons' first game of the season was scheduled for an evening in early May. Since this particular league included grades six through eight, our older son was a third-year veteran on the team, while his younger brother, a sixth-grader, was among the new recruits. The usual crowd of parents had gathered as I took my seat on a weather-beaten plank, third row from the top. Sandwiched between a cotton-candy-faced youngster and somebody's mother, I checked the scoreboard. Fourth inning already. Because the boys had anticipated my late arrival they instructed me to watch the first base and catcher positions. As my attention moved between them, I glanced at the pitcher's mound. Jason Voldner?

Jason was undoubtedly the most well-liked and good-natured boy on the team, but athletically, his participation had been limited to the alternating positions of right field or bench—the latter, unfortunately, more frequently. Having spent an uncountable number of hours as a spectator (on an equally uncountable number of varying bleachers), it is my belief that every ball field has its own version of Jason Voldner.

The Jasons of the world show up at a tender young age for their first Saturday morning T-ball practice, oiled glove in hand. By the end of this long awaited "chance to play ball," the heavy-hearted Jasons return home remembering the boy who hit farther, the boy who ran faster and the boy who actually knew what he was supposed to do with the glove.

Ability is not only recognized but utilized, allowing for the exceptional players to become even more so, while the Jasons wait their turn to play the seventh inning. Right field. Their allotted playing time is not only limited, it's conditional: only if the team is already winning. If not, the Jasons have simply been waiting to go home. And yet here was Jason Voldner pitching what I would say was the game of his life.

Turning to comment to anyone willing to listen, I now realized that the "somebody's mother" sitting beside me belonged to Jason. "Such talent," I offered. "I've never seen your son pitch before." In a voice of quiet resolve she responded, "Neither have I." And then she told me this story.

Four weeks ago, she had chauffeured a car full of boys, her son included, to this same baseball diamond for their first spring practice. Just before dusk she had sat on her porch swing, dodging the sudden downpour and waiting for the next carpool mother to drop Jason off after practice. As the van pulled up, Jason emerged from behind the sliding door. "His face was a combination of dirt smudges and rain streaks and would have masked from anyone but me that he was upset," she said.

"My immediate concern was for an injury," Jason's mother continued. But there was none. Probing questions led her no closer to the elusive pain. By bedtime, she knew no more than she did back on the porch. This would change shortly.

"Sometime in the hours that followed, I was awakened by choking sobs. Jason's. At his bedside, broken words were telling his story. 'Waiting. Eighth grade. Sick of right field. Eighth grade.'" As Jason's mother calmed her son, he further explained that Matthew, a sixth-grader, was going to play second-base "because his dad is coaching"; John, a sixth-grader, was assigned to shortstop "because he's Matthew's friend"; and Brian, yet another sixth-grader, was the new catcher "because his brother is on the team."

I found myself bristling here and wondered where her story was going. Brian was my younger son.

"Not fair. Not fair. Not fair." Listening to Jason, his mother's heart ached for him. There should be a word that takes empathy to another level; a word for the exclusive use of parents.

"While my son was waiting for me to agree with him," said his mother, "I was making the difficult decision not to. One has to be careful when having a direct and lasting effect on another person's negative emotions. Agreement may appear to be the most caring and loyal means of help, but in reality, it can work to the contrary as you reinforce the negative feelings.

"So first I explained to Jason that until we were ready to assist the coach with his responsibilities, we would trust his judgments.

"Secondly, I reminded him how seldom we passed the vacant lot on the corner of our block without finding the three sixth-graders in question involved in a random, unscheduled game of ball. Playing infield is not about being in the sixth grade or the eighth; it's about working hard and capability, not preferential treatment. All through your life you are going to come into contact with individuals possessing a natural talent for what they are pursuing—on the ballfield, in the classroom, in the workplace. Does this mean you are unable to achieve what they have? Certainly not. You simply have to choose to work harder. Resentment, blame and excuses only poison potential."

Finally, Jason's mother tucked him back into bed. As she smoothed the covers over him, she said to her son, "You're disappointed that the coach doesn't believe in you, Jason, but before you can expect others to believe in you, you have to believe in yourself. The coach is basing his placements on the performance he has seen thus far. If you truly feel you deserve a position other than right field, then prove it." With those words she kissed him goodnight.

Jason's mother laughed softly. "We spoke more in those few minutes than we have pretty much in the weeks since. Our contact recently has been through notes that Jason leaves me on the kitchen table: 'Gone to practice. Gone to prove it.'" She paused. "And he did."

Yes, it has been my experience that one stumbles across life's most profound lessons in the most unexpected places—like the neighborhood Little League baseball diamond, while sitting on a weather-beaten plank, third row from the top.

CAUGHT ANY YET?

Spring and opening day of the fishing season rarely arrive at the same time in northern Wisconsin. Early one morning my dad rousted us kids out of bed. We trekked three miles through the dark, cold woods. When we reached the lake, we threw out our lines and waited. And waited. As the sun rose, we saw immediately why we hadn't caught any fish. There lay all our hooks, carefully baited—on a solid sheet of ice.

HELEN F. DUPLAYEE

FROM *READER'S DIGEST*

RELEASING THE ARROW

STU WEBER

FROM *TENDER WARRIOR*

As I write these words, I'm looking at three arrows on my desk. They differ from one another. Any archer could see that at a glance. Yet in other ways they are remarkably similar.

I'm turning one in my hand, now. Feeling the heft and balance of its shaft. Looking down its length to the round edges of its blunt head. It's a target arrow, and a good one. I wouldn't waste my time with anything less. It has plastic vanes instead of feathers—the kind of arrow you'd want for shooting in rainy western Oregon. This second one now...yes, it has a good feel to it, too. A hunting arrow. Smooth shaft. Well balanced. A slightly heavier head, and crafted to a literal razor's edge. It's a "broadhead." Plastic-vaned and intended for wet country hunting. The third one is the kind I carry east of the mountains, over on the dry side. It's basically a twin of the second arrow, but it sports neat black and gray feathers instead of plastic.

They're different, these arrows of mine. Each intended for a different impact. Each designed for a different sort of target. They're also very similar; each has been fashioned and crafted, molded and balanced. They're all intended for flight. They're all intended for a target. They're all intended for maximum impact on that target.

They're good arrows. But then again, they're not much better than the archer who notches them on the bow. They're not much better than the fullness of his draw. They're not much better than the smoothness of his release. No matter how finely crafted those arrows might be, you couldn't pull a guy off the street and expect him to let loose with a seventy-pound bow and nail a target with one of them. Accuracy demands a trained, full draw and a disciplined release.

As I write these words, I'm looking at a picture on my desk.

It's a picture of my three sons—Kent, Blake, and Ryan. They're different, these sons of mine. Unbelievably different. But they're also similar.

Each was crafted by the Lord God in the secret place of his mother's womb. And each was fashioned, balanced, and readied for flight within the four walls of our home.

My three arrows were all designed to leap from the bow and split the air. I enjoy bow hunting, and I intend to use these arrows—whether on a cedar bale target or on a bull elk stamping on some back-country ridge on a frosty morning. These arrows aren't for show. They were never intended to stay in the quiver. The quiver is just a vehicle that carries them until they are ready for release. You might say those arrows were made to be released. They were made to play. They were made to pierce a target.

So it is with my three sons. They were never intended to stay bunched in the four walls of their childhood home. Yes, the home is a vehicle to fashion and straighten and true and balance those boys. But when the moment comes…young men—and young women—were made to experience flight.

CONFESSIONS TO A BENCH COACH

VICKEY BANKS

He was tired. It had been a long day in a long week. The kind of day when all he wanted to do was go home and collapse into his recliner with the television remote control at his disposal. An earlier glance at his schedule had told him it wasn't to be—not tonight anyway. Tonight he would be in a small, stuffy elementary gymnasium. Noise would bounce off of each and every wall while a group of overexcited six-year-old boys would be holding him responsible for their happiness.

Keith looked at the disorderly piles on his desk and let out a sigh. Opening his briefcase, he began to pack up his work for the day. It was time for him to take off his tie and put on his tennis shoes. It was time for him to become Hayden's dad, bench coach for the Rockets basketball team.

The primary job description for the bench coach of this rowdy group was to maintain some semblance of order and to monitor the playing time of each and every boy. Herein lay the problem: they didn't want order and they weren't interested in being monitored! One or two were so bold as to roll their eyes and let out a not-so-quiet groan when Keith pulled them out to take their turn on the bench. *I don't need this stress,* Keith thought, and smiled to himself.

Finally, it was Matthew's turn to sit out. Matthew had been a problem all season. He didn't pay attention. He disobeyed directions like he had never even heard them. On more than one occasion, he had looked right at Keith or the head coach and totally discounted their instructions. He never said much; he just did his own thing.

Tonight was different. Tonight Matthew talked.

"That's not really my Dad," he said matter-of-factly, looking in the direction of the man who had brought him to the game. "He's really my Granddad. My dad is in jail because he did some really bad things."

As Keith listened to this unprovoked admission, it hit him. *No, he didn't need this stress, but maybe Matthew needed him.* Suddenly, the job description of a bench coach changed.

In golf as in life it's the follow-through that makes the difference.

ANONYMOUS

INTEGRITY

DENIS WAITLEY

FROM *BEING THE BEST*

Some time ago, an article in *National Racquetball* magazine told the story of Reuben Gonzales, who was in the final match of a professional racquetball tournament. It was Gonzales' first shot at a victory on the pro circuit, and he was playing the perennial champion.

In the fourth and final game, at match point, Gonzales made a super "kill" shot into the front wall to win it all. The referee called it good. One of the two linesmen affirmed that the shot was in.

But Gonzales, after a moment's hesitation, turned around, shook his opponent's hand, and declared that his shot had "skipped" into the wall, hitting the court floor first. As a result, he lost the match. He walked off the court. Everybody was stunned.

The next issue of *National Racquetball* magazine displayed Reuben Gonzales on its front cover. The story searched for an explanation of this first-ever occurrence on the professional racquetball circuit.

Who could ever imagine it in any sport or endeavor? A player, with everything officially in his favor, with victory in hand, disqualified *himself* at match point and lost!

When asked why he did it, Reuben said, "It was the only thing I could do to maintain my integrity."

LEGACY

A SPLENDID TORCH

I want to be thoroughly used up when I die,
for the harder I work, the more I live,
Life is no brief candle for me.
It is a sort of splendid torch which
I have got hold of for a moment,
and I want to make it burn as brightly
as possible before handing it on
to future generations.

GEORGE BERNARD SHAW

A SINGLE CROCUS

JOAN ANDERSON

FROM *WHERE WONDERS PREVAIL*

I t was an autumn morning shortly after my husband and I moved into our first house. Our children were upstairs unpacking, and I was look-ing out the window at my father moving around mysteriously on the front lawn. My parents lived nearby, and Dad had visited us several times already. "What are you doing out there?" I called to him.

He looked up, smiling. "I'm making you a surprise." Knowing my father, I thought it could be just about anything. A self-employed jobber, he was always building things out of odds and ends. When we were kids, he once rigged up a jungle gym out of wheels and pulleys. For one of my Halloween parties, he created an electrical pumpkin and mounted it on a broomstick. As guests came to our door, he would light the pumpkin and have it pop out in front of them from a hiding place in the bushes.

Today, however, Dad would say no more, and caught up in the busy-ness of our new life, I eventually forgot about his surprise.

Until one raw day the following March when I glanced out the win-dow. Dismal. Overcast. Little piles of dirty snow still stubbornly littering the lawn. Would winter ever end?

And yet…was it a mirage? I strained to see what I thought was some-thing pink, miraculously peeking out of a drift. And was that a dot of blue across the yard, a small note of optimism in this gloomy expanse? I grabbed my coat and headed outside for a closer look.

They were crocuses, scattered whimsically throughout the front lawn. Lavender, blue, yellow and my favorite pink—little faces bobbing in the bitter wind.

Dad, I smiled, remembering the bulbs he had secretly planted last fall. He knew how the darkness and dreariness of winter always got me down. What could have been more perfectly timed, more attuned to my needs? How blessed I was, not only for the flowers but for him.

My father's crocuses bloomed each spring for the next four or five seasons, bringing that same assurance every time they arrived: *Hard times almost over. Hold on, keep going, light is coming soon.*

Then a spring came with only half the usual blooms. The next spring there were none. I missed the crocuses, but my life was busier than ever, and I had never been much of a gardener. I would ask Dad to come over and plant new bulbs. But I never did.

He died suddenly one October day. My family grieved deeply, leaning on our faith. I missed him terribly, though I knew he would always be a part of us.

Four years passed, and on a dismal spring afternoon I was running errands and found myself feeling depressed. You've got the winter blahs again, I told myself. You get them every year; it's chemistry. But it was something else too.

It was Dad's birthday, and I found myself thinking about him. This was not unusual—my family often talked about him, remembering how he lived his faith. Once I saw him take off his coat and give it to a homeless man. Often he'd chat with strangers passing by his storefront, and if he learned they were poor and hungry, he would invite them home for a meal. But now, in the car, I couldn't help wondering, *How* is he now? *Where* is he? Is there really a heaven?

I felt guilty for having doubts, but sometimes, I thought as I turned into our driveway, faith is so hard.

Suddenly I slowed, stopped and stared at the lawn. Muddy grass and small gray mounds of melting snow. And there, bravely waving in the wind, was one pink crocus.

How could a flower bloom from a bulb more than 18 years old, one that had not blossomed in over a decade? But there was the crocus. Tears filled my eyes as I realized its significance.

Hold on, keep going, light is coming soon. The pink crocus bloomed for only a day. But it built my faith for a lifetime.

(Reprinted with permission from the April 1998 *Reader's Digest.*)

DAD'S MARK

BILL HYBELS

FROM *HONEST TO GOD?*

Recently my brother and I spent a lunch hour discussing the mark our dad left on our lives. Dad wasn't a perfect man, but he was authentically masculine. He loved God deeply and knew how to be firm yet compassionate.

Dan and I reminisced about the times we had sailed with him on Lake Michigan. We remembered violent storms with fifty-mile-an-hour winds. All the other sailors would dash for the harbor, but Dad would smile from ear to ear and say, "Let's head out farther!"

We talked about the tough business decisions we had seen him make. We winced when we remembered his firm hand of discipline that blocked our rebellious streaks. We never doubted it. Dad was strong, tough, and thoroughly masculine.

Yet for twenty-five years he spent nearly every Sunday afternoon standing in front of a hundred mentally retarded women at the state mental hospital. Gently and patiently he led them in a song service. Few of them could even sing, but he didn't care. He knew it made them feel loved. Afterward he stood by the door while each of those disheveled, broken women planted kisses on his cheek. As little guys, Dan and I had the unspeakable privilege of watching our six-foot-three, two-hundred-twenty-pound, thoroughly masculine dad treat these forgotten women with a gentleness that marked us.

If you're a dad, what kind of mark are you leaving on your children, especially your sons? Do you realize that your little boys are watching you like hawks? They're trying to figure out what maleness is all about, and you're their model. I hope they see in you a deep, uncompromising love for God. I hope they see both toughness and tenderness. If they do, then you have served them well; they will be forever grateful.

RESOLUTIONS

Choose to love—rather than hate
Choose to smile—rather than frown
Choose to build—rather than destroy
Choose to persevere—rather than quit
Choose to praise—rather than gossip
Choose to heal—rather than wound
Choose to give—rather than grasp
Choose to act—rather than delay
Choose to forgive—rather than curse
Choose to pray—rather than despair.

AUTHOR UNKNOWN

EXCHANGING GIFTS

CATHY DOWNS

FROM *THE READING TEACHER*

My father was one of those old-fashioned country preachers who spouted verses from the pulpit of the Baptist church and made the listeners tremble in their seats. At other times he recited chapters from John without ever glancing at the Bible clutched in his hand.

One afternoon after school, my father and I were driving down an old dirt road to visit one of the elderly ladies of the church. I had just received my new third-grade reader. It was my first real hardback book and I was so proud of it. I had already read one story to my father and was starting another one, when I came to a word that I did not know. I held the book up so Father could see it and asked him what the word was. He mumbled something about not being able to read and drive at the same time, so very slowly I spelled the word: "a-u-t-u-m-n." My father drove on in silence. Angry, I yelled at him, "Can't you read?"

My father pulled the car over to the side of the road and turned off the ignition. "No, Cathy, I can't read," he whispered softly. "No, I can't read."

He reached over and took my new book out of my hand. "I can't read anything in this book," he said with such pain that even I, a small third-grade child, could feel it.

Very quietly, my father began to talk of his childhood, of the big family that survived by the physical labor that was expected of everyone in the family. If crops were ready to be harvested, school and books could wait. Cotton had to be hoed in the summer and picked in the fall. In the winter, animals had to be slaughtered and preserved. There were many mouths to feed, and everyone had to pull his or her load. To make life even more difficult, my father had two brothers who were handicapped, so the others had to double up and carry the load.

As a result of his excessive absences from school, my father failed several grades. His motivation to learn evaporated, and at the age of 16, he dropped out of school.

I will never forget the sorrow in my father's voice as he told me about his childhood. I will also never forget the shame in his voice when he talked about how hard it was for him never to have been able to help his five children with their lessons in school. I never loved my father more than I did at that moment.

I remembered then how Father could read so well when he was in the pulpit, how he read entire chapters at one time without ever missing a word. It was then that I also realized what a truly remarkable man he was. He was able to listen to my mother read something several times and then recite it verbatim from memory. What an incredible memory!

It was then that I became a reading teacher. I vowed that I would teach my father to read. Whatever my teacher did with me at school, I did with my father. I taught him the sounds and patterns of language as I learned them. When I read a story at school, I came home and taught my father to read it. When I struggled with a new concept, he struggled along with me. In return, he helped me find mnemonic devices to memorize items that I needed to pass tests. Soon he learned to write simple stories and poems. Then he was able to write quotations and jot down notes he needed for his sermons. The proudest moment of my life came when my father read the Scripture—really read it for his Sunday sermon.

Father never lost his fascination with the written language. He read everything he could get his hands on. He was very proud the summer he could read the *Farmer's Almanac* to my mother and give her advice on how to plant the garden.

My father was diagnosed with terminal lung cancer in 1977 and died nine months later. During those nine months, he read the Bible from Genesis through Revelation. His proudest moment was when he closed the Bible, knowing he could read all that was written inside it.

Before my father died, he thanked me for the gift that I had given him. He didn't realize, however, the gift that he had given me: I knew that just as he had been called to be a pastor, I had been called to be a reading teacher. Because of my father, I believe that if I can spare one child the heartache and humiliation of illiteracy, my career as a teacher is wholly worthwhile. Thank you, Father.

DOING WHAT
OUR FATHER SAYS

LUIS PALAU

FROM *DEVOTIONS #2*

More than ninety people conducted an all-night search for Dominic DeCarlo, an eight-year-old boy lost on a snowy mountain slope. Dominic, who had been on a skiing trip with his father, apparently had ridden on a new lift and skied off the run without realizing it.

As each hour passed, the search party and the boy's family became more and more concerned for his health and safety. By dawn they had found no trace of the boy. Two helicopter crews joined the search, and within fifteen minutes they spotted ski tracks. A ground team followed the tracks, which changed to small footprints. The footprints led to a tree, where they found the boy at last.

"He's in super shape!" Sergeant Terry Silbaugh, area search-and-rescue coordinator, announced to the anxious family and press. "In fact, he's in better shape than we are right now!" A hospital spokeswoman said the boy was in fine condition, so he wasn't even admitted.

Silbaugh explained why the boy did so well despite spending a night in the freezing elements: His father had enough forethought to warn the boy what to do if he became lost, and his son had enough trust to do exactly what his father said.

Dominic protected himself from possible frostbite and hypothermia by snuggling up to a tree and covering himself with branches. As a young child, he never would have thought of doing this on his own. He was simply obeying his wise and loving father.

I've thought of Dominic many times. He's a great illustration of the positive, life-changing influence a father can have on his child. My own father died when I was only a little older than Dominic. Yet no one else has had a more profound influence on the course and direction of my life.

I practically idolized my father as a boy. I loved to say my name was "Luis Palau Jr." He was my ideal of a man, even though he was quiet and humble for a person of such stature in the church and community. His pride in the Gospel and boldness to share it with others marked my life.

My dad was consistent, the same person at home as he was at church. He rose early on cold winter mornings to start a wood fire in the stove. I should have been sleeping, but often I sneaked out of bed just to watch him putter around the house.

If I watched long enough, I might see him go into his office—a little study he built on one side of the house—and kneel alone. In those days we didn't have central heating, so he would wrap himself in a blanket or poncho. Then he would read the Bible and pray before going out to work. Though I was not even seven years old yet, I would steal back to my bed, feeling warm and grateful that I had a good dad.

One day he told me that he read a chapter from Proverbs every day, since it has thirty-one chapters and there are thirty-one days in most months. His example stuck with me, and I still try to practice it. I have told so many friends and associates that story that many, many people now do the same. In spite of the other Bible studying and reading I do, I try to start the day with my chapter from Proverbs. And many a time I read it on my knees.

My father's memory has marked my life for good. Thank God for good dads!

BETWEEN THE LINES

CHARLOTTE ADELSPERGER

After a moving memorial service for my beloved father, Walter Rist, our family gathered at our childhood home to be with Mother. Memories of Dad whirled in my mind. I could see his warm brown eyes and contagious smile. I envisioned all six-foot-four of him in hat and coat, headed to teach his classes at the college. Quickly, a new scene flashed in my mind of Dad in a T-shirt playing ball with Alberta, Wally, and me on the front lawn. He was swinging a baseball bat, hitting long flies to us kids—years ago.

But special memories couldn't push away the dark shadows of separation from the one we loved.

Later in the evening, while looking for something in a closet, we found a paper sack marked, "Charlotte's Scrapbook." In curiosity, I opened it. There it was—my "Inspiration from Here and There" scrapbook I had kept as a teenager. I had forgotten all about it until this moment when I leafed through the pages of pasted pictures from magazines and church bulletins. They were punctuated with clippings of famous quotes, Bible verses, and poetry. *This was me as a teenager,* I thought. *My heart's desires.*

Then I saw something I'd never seen before—my father's handwriting

penciled on page after page! My throat tightened as I read the little notes
Dad had slipped in to communicate with me. They were love messages
and words of wisdom. I had no idea when he had written these, but *this*
was the day to find them!

On the first page, Dad wrote, "Life is never a burden if love prevails."
My chin quivered. I trembled. I could hardly believe the timeliness of his
words. I flipped the pages for more.

Under a picture of a bride being given away by her father, my dad
wrote, "How proud I was to walk down the aisle with you, Charlotte!"

Near a copy of the Lord's Prayer he had scrawled, "I have always
found the strength I needed, but only with God's help. He has never failed
me." What a comfort!

I turned to a picture of a young boy sitting on the grass with a gentle
collie resting its head on his lap. Beneath it were these words, "I had a collie like this one when I was a boy. She was run over by a streetcar and disappeared. Three weeks later she came home, limping with a broken leg,
her tail cut off. Her name was Queenie. She lived for many more years. I
watched her give birth to seven puppies. I loved her very much.—Dad."

My moist eyes blurred as I read another page. "Dear Charlotte, listen
to your children! Let them talk. Hold Bob's hand whenever you can. Hold
your children's hands. Much love will be transferred, much warmth to
remember." What a treasure of guidance for me as a wife and mother! I
clung to the words from my dad whose gentle big hand often held mine.

In those moments of paging through the scrapbook, incredible comfort was etched on the gray canvas of my life. On this, the day my father
was buried, he had a loving "last word." Such a precious surprise, somehow allowed by God, cast victorious light on the shadows of my grief. I
was able to walk on, covered by fresh beacons of strength.

WHAT YOU
REMEMBER MOST

STEVEN J. LAWSON

FROM *THE LEGACY*

Howard Hendricks, one of my professors at Dallas Seminary years ago, told us a story one day in class that I've never forgotten. He told us about twin boys who were former students who stopped by his office after class one day to talk. During the course of the conversation, Hendricks asked them about their father, a prominent Christian leader, "Guys, what do you remember most about your dad as you were growing up?"

After a short pause, one of the young men said, "I'll never forget the times he would spend wrestling with us on the floor. Even as teenagers, he would clear out the den furniture and roll around the floor laughing with us."

The other son reflected, "What I remember most about my dad was, when we were in high school, I threw a paper route and I would have to get up early in the morning to deliver the paper. Each morning, I'd walk past my dad's bedroom door and it would be cracked open. I'd see him in there down on his knees and I knew he was praying for us. That's what I remember most about my dad."

Then "Prof" Hendricks delivered the punch. He leaned across the podium, peered over the top of his glasses, and asked the penetrating question, "By the way, what will your kids remember you for?"

LEGACY OF LOVE

JANE LANDIN RAMIREZ
FROM *IT'S JUST ABOUT CHRISTMAS*

I t was an early October morning—and as usual, I rushed about to get our second grader, Kevin, and fifth grader, Joe, ready for school and myself ready for work. Since my husband, Sandy, had the morning off, he was busy making breakfast for everyone.

"Daddy, can you take us to school today?" asked Kevin.

"'Fraid not, Bunbun. Your daddy's gonna work off some pounds today on his bike." He turned to me and winked. "I want that new suit your mom bought me to fit just right."

Sandy had just been promoted to assistant manager at work, and we were all proud of him. "Don't forget, I'm taking my special girl out tonight for a celebration dinner," he added.

Sandy had always been a romantic. He had won my heart our freshman year in high school with his homemade valentine, and twenty years later, he could still make me blush.

"Bye, Dad. Be careful on your bike," said Joe, as we walked out to the car.

"See you soon! I love you," Sandy said, waving to us from the front door.

I dropped the boys off at school and hurried to the office. My morning was so busy, I decided to work through lunch. *Nothing's going to keep me from leaving on time today!* I thought.

But shortly before three o'clock, a coworker and close friend, Rose, entered my office. "Jane, there's been an accident," she said, ashen faced. "Sandy's at the hospital."

"How bad is it? Why didn't someone call me? What hospital is he at? Who called you?" I asked, panic-stricken.

"Calm down, Jane. I don't know how badly he's hurt. His boss called me. Someone from the hospital called him. I'll drive you there," she said.

My heart pounded as I went up to the front desk of the emergency room and asked to see my husband.

The attendant telephoned someone. "His wife is here," he said quietly, then turned to me. "Someone is coming to talk to you. Please wait here."

"Is he all right? Where is he? Can I see him?"

"Please wait here, ma'am. Someone will be here soon," he pleaded.

The hospital chaplain arrived and quietly ushered me into a private waiting room. "Your husband's been with us since nine-thirty this morning. We were told by the ambulance attendants he was hit by a car while riding a bicycle. The doctor will be here soon to talk to you. Is there someone I could call for you?"

This is a bad dream—I'll wake up from it soon, I thought, dazed and speechless. Just then, Rose entered the room. Her worried face triggered the tears I was fighting back. She sat me down and took over calling my family and our pastor. "Your sister is bringing the boys," she said.

I jumped to my feet when the doctor entered the room. "I'm Dr. Gray. Your husband is in ICU. I'm afraid the news isn't good. He suffered severe trauma to the head and spine. We had to amputate his left leg to control the bleeding. He's not breathing on his own, and the blood supply to his brain is about 2 percent of the normal level. His injuries were so severe, it's a miracle he's hung on as long as he has. I'm sorry—there's nothing more we can do."

My legs collapsed. I had to be helped to a chair. Anger and guilt consumed me, and I lashed out, "He's been alone all this time! Why did you wait so long to call me?"

The chaplain responded, "Your husband wasn't carrying any ID, so the police had only the initials from his high school ring to go on. One of our nurses identified him from the yearbook and remembered where he worked. His boss told us he would try to locate you. I'm sorry it took so long to contact you."

"Please take me to him," I said, forcing down the lump in my throat.

"He never regained consciousness. His injuries have distorted his features, and all the tubing going through his body may be shocking," explained Dr. Gray.

"I need to see him right now," I insisted. I followed Dr. Gray. Tears welled in my eyes as I approached Sandy. I caressed his cold hands and gently kissed his forehead. "I'm here, my love. I'm so sorry that I didn't get here sooner," I said softly. Thoughts raced through my mind: *I'm so afraid—I don't know if I can go on without Sandy. I feel so alone. Please help me, Lord. Why did this have to happen? I feel so helpless. Dear God, please spare him any further suffering. Lord, help me to be strong for the boys.*

"I love you," I whispered. "You're in God's hands now." I so wanted Sandy to open his eyes and tell me everything would be all right.

Our silence was broken by a tap on my shoulder. Dr. Gray asked me to follow him. Outside the room were two other people.

"Mrs. Martinez, I know this is an extremely difficult time for you," said Dr. Gray. "I wish there were an easier way to do this, but there's very little time. Your husband's heart and other vital organs weren't injured by the accident, and there are two people here from an organ bank. They'd like a few minutes with you."

"Please, Dr. Gray, are you sure there's no hope?"

He replied sympathetically, "I wish I could tell you what you want to hear. Please listen to what these people have to say."

I'd never given organ donation any serious thought. Sandy and I'd never discussed it, and the idea was a bit frightening. But I listened as they gently asked me if we'd consider the possibility of donating Sandy's organs. Everything was happening so fast, I was relieved to see our pastor arrive.

Reverend O'Connor followed me into Sandy's room. "Sandy isn't going to make it, and those people were talking to me about donating his organs. I don't know what to do," I said.

"Jane, Sandy's work in the church exemplified his caring, giving nature. Remembering that may help you decide what to do. It's a decision, however, you shouldn't make alone. Do the boys know what's happening?" he added.

"No, they're on their way. I don't know how I'm going to explain all this to them," I said as we both returned to the waiting room.

The crowded waiting room became a silent blur of faces when I entered. Two frightened little boys raced to me.

"Where's Daddy, Mommy? Why can't we see him?" they both asked.

I led them by the hand to Sandy's room. They stared at the figure on the bed as if he were a stranger. "Daddy is very hurt. He was struck by a car and thrown from his bike. He hit his head very hard. Don't be afraid."

We all huddled in a tight embrace, and I began, "Boys, the doctors have done everything to try to help him. We all love him very much, and I know you both want him to get better."

"Yes, Mommy, but how can we help him?" asked Kevin.

"The doctors can't help him, and we can't help him, but there is someone who can help him," I said.

"You mean God, don't you, Mommy?" asked Joe.

"Yes, God can help him, but to do that, he needs to take Daddy to heaven to live with him," I answered.

"But then we won't see him anymore, like Grandpa," sobbed Kevin.

"Daddy will always be with us, Kevin. He's in our hearts, and because we love him so much, we need to let him go to heaven where he won't hurt anymore. Grandpa's already in heaven, so Daddy won't be alone. Someday, when we go to heaven, we'll see both of them again," I explained.

"Do you remember how Daddy was always helping other people?" I added.

"Yes, Daddy liked helping people, even people he didn't know," added Kevin.

"Do you think Daddy would want to continue helping people if he could?" I asked.

"I guess so, but how, Mommy?" asked Joe.

"In heaven, God will give Daddy a new body that doesn't hurt, so he won't need his old body anymore. There are people we could help feel better if we gave them Daddy's beautiful green eyes or his great big heart," I explained.

"Will Daddy still love us even if he doesn't have his old heart? Will he still remember us?" questioned Kevin.

"Of course he will. Daddy will always love us no matter what happens," I answered.

After a brief silence, Kevin spoke. "Let's help those people, Mommy. Daddy would want us to."

Joe remained silent a few minutes longer. Cuddling his father's hand between his two small hands, he kissed it and whispered, "I love you, Daddy. Tell Grandpa I love him, too." Then he quietly slipped out of the room.

The rest of the family supported our decision without hesitation. My hands trembled as I signed the consent papers. After giving all the family some quick time alone with Sandy, the surgeons went to work to save all the organs possible.

As my sister drove me home, I thought of the celebration dinner that would never be and the new suit that would now be worn for the first and last time.

The healing process that followed was made easier with each letter received from an organ bank. Although the identities of the recipients were concealed, we read about the high school principal who was within hours of dying until he received Sandy's heart. We heard from the kidney foundation about the two people who were now free from their dialysis machines. Two elderly persons received the gift of sight through cornea transplants. Sharing the letters with Kevin and Joe made it easier to talk about our loss.

Two months after the accident, we faced our first Christmas without Sandy. "Mommy, who's gonna put our Christmas lights up this year?" Kevin repeatedly asked.

I knew I couldn't disappoint the boys and break a family tradition of decorating our home with Christmas lights, but I just couldn't get into the Christmas spirit. Then it came—a letter from the organ tissue bank. As I read it aloud, the boys listened intently: "Your generous gift of life has shed light on the lives of some one hundred burn patients and their families, some with very severe skin burns."

"Mom, Daddy's been gone a long time, and he's still helping people," Joe said proudly.

"Mommy, I don't think that letter is right. Daddy was a very big man. I can't believe he only helped one hundred people. He probably helped at least a million!" Kevin added.

Memories of past Christmases flashed through my mind. Sandy always played Santa at our family gatherings. The old Santa suit didn't need much padding, and his naturally jolly cheeks and *ho ho ho's* brought laughter to all. He would be missed deeply—particularly this first Christmas—and not only by his family. There'd be one less volunteer this year to deliver food and gifts to the needy or serve guests hot meals at the Ronald McDonald House. A beautiful sympathy card made and signed by the students from his Sunday school class reflected the love they had for their teacher. One child had written, "I am not going to be sad, because Mr. Martinez always made me laugh."

Christmas is a joyous season, I reflected. Like the child from his class, I, too, would refuse to be sad. Sandy had touched the lives of many—and even now his legacy of helping others was very much alive. I could not—and would not—let him down.

With renewed vigor, I exclaimed, "Boys, what do you say we get started on those lights and make Daddy proud of us, too!"

THE POWER
OF BEING THERE

THOM HUNTER

FROM *THOSE NOT-SO-STILL SMALL VOICES*

While growing up, I had no father at home. So my goal when *I* grew up was to be a daddy. Not just a father—I had a father somewhere. I didn't have a daddy.

The No. 1 responsibility of a daddy, I told myself, is to "be there," not to miss the events, momentous and miniature, that bind father to son. All my life I catalogued events I would have shared with my daddy. "Someday," I vowed, "I'll enjoy these with *my* children."

Somedays usually arrive when we are least prepared—bogged down in work, over-scheduled and fatigued. In the midst of making to-do lists, I hear a small voice zeroing in, "You *will* be there, won't you, Daddy?"

"Of course," I answer, clearing my throat. "Wouldn't miss it."

The year was 1984, the busiest of my adult life. The year after the birth of our fourth son. The year of my firstborn's first-grade picnic.

I almost did miss the picnic, drowning in my deadlines. But I fled from the office just in time and sped to the park.

Zachary sat hunched over in the grass near the picnic table. The sun beat down on his brown neck poking out of his T-shirt. He was dirty from the playground, scraped on both elbows, and sweaty. His socks hung limply over the top of once-white tennis shoes. He sat alone surrounded by 1000—or at least 75—seven-year-olds.

Zach's eyes were following something intently as it journeyed through the tall grass. It was a goldish, shiny bug. When the fleeing creature would almost get beyond his reach, he would throw out a finger roadblock.

"Oh, good," he said, as I sat down beside him. "I was afraid you wouldn't get here before the gold bug got away. Look."

He said "before" the gold bug got away, I thought. Zach had never imagined that I might not show up, that I might have forgotten the Washington School picnic. It was a once-only moment in his life.

Surrounded by moms, Zachary and I ate our sandwiches, sitting in the grass together, my legs cramping, my knee joints stiffening. He pointed out various kids and told me their names. He introduced me to Rachel, whom he chases and who chases him. Every now and then a child would drift by and ask Zach in hushed tones, "Is that your dad?"

Each time I wanted to lose 40 pounds on the spot, change into a sporty tennis outfit and flex my muscles to give Zach something to be proud of. But Zach looked right at me, just as I was, and beamed. "He sure is."

Zach shared his Chiclets with me. He had a hard time believing I chewed Chiclets way back when I was seven.

"Did you share them with your dad?" he asked. I couldn't answer, so I changed the subject.

That evening, after we both got home, I lifted Zachary up to look into the bird's nest on the front porch. I was amazed at how heavy a seven-year-old is.

He peeked inside the nest. No eggs yet, but some grass and feathers waiting.

"Did your dad ever lift you up to see inside a bird's nest?" he asked. Once again, I couldn't answer.

Later, in his room, decorated with the heroes and dreams of his young life, I tucked him in for the night. He lay on his stomach, and I rubbed his back until his eyes closed. Only when I got to the door did I find out he was just pretending to sleep, as he shouted out, "Good-night, Daddy!"

Over the years, I have stashed away a valuable collection of "being theres." I share them often with my children, pulling them out when doubts appear, using them to close gaps and heal hurts. There is great power in "remember whens," but you can use them only if you have them.

Someday Zachary's son or daughter will ask him, "Did your daddy ever lift you up to see inside a bird's nest?"

I'm glad he will have an answer.

(Reprinted with permission from the April 1995 *Reader's Digest*.)

MEMORIES

DENNIS RAINEY

FROM *PULLING WEEDS, PLANTING SEEDS*

I nstead of just things, my dad gave me imperishable memories. Little league baseball the three years he was my coach. Fishing trips where he netted my fish. A "clipped" collection of all the baseball and basketball scores from my games, of which he never missed one. There are memories of watching him through the frosted window of our old pickup truck as he delivered hams at Christmas. Memories of the feel of his whiskers when he wrestled with me on the floor of the living room. Memories of him whispering to me, an extroverted, impetuous boy, not to bother people while they work. And memories of snuggling close to him as we watched the baseball game of the week on television with Dizzy Dean as the announcer.

As an impressionable young boy, my radar caught more of his life than he ever knew. During my perilous teenage years he was the model and hero I needed—and he still is. He taught me the importance of hard work and completing a task. I learned about lasting commitment from him—I never feared my parents would divorce. My dad was absolutely committed to my mom. I felt secure and protected.

Most importantly, he taught me about *character.* He did what was right, even when no one was looking. I never heard him talk about cheating on taxes—he paid them and didn't grumble. His integrity was impeccable. I never heard him lie, and his eyes always demanded the same truth in return. The mental image of his character still fuels and energizes my life today.

"Dad's home!" I can still hear the door slam, and feel the house quake.

This morning as I write this, Dad truly is "home"—in heaven. I look forward to seeing him again someday and thanking him for the legacy he gave me.

But right now, you'll have to pardon me—I miss him.

PURPOSE AND DESTINY

Keep a clear eye toward life's end. Do not forget your purpose and destiny as God's creature. What you are in his sight is what you are and nothing more. Remember that when you leave this earth, you can take with you nothing that you have received—fading symbols of honor, trappings of power—but only what you have given: a full heart enriched by honest service, love, sacrifice, and courage.

FRANCIS OF ASSISI

MY DAD

CHARLES SWINDOLL
FROM *COME BEFORE WINTER*

y dad died last night.

He left like he had lived. Quietly. Graciously. With dignity. Without demands or harsh words or even a frown, he surrendered himself—a tired, frail, humble gentleman—into the waiting arms of his Savior. Death, selfish and cursed enemy of man, won another battle.

As I stroked the hair from his forehead and kissed him goodbye, a hundred boyhood memories played around in my head.

♦ When I learned to ride a bike, he was there.

♦ When I wrestled with the multiplication tables, his quick wit erased the hassle.

♦ When I discovered the adventure of driving a car, he was near, encouraging me.

♦ When I got my first job (delivering newspapers), he informed me how to increase my subscriptions and win the prize. It worked!

♦ When I did a hitch in the Marine Corps, the discipline I had learned from him made the transition easier.

From him I learned to seine for shrimp. How to gig flounder and catch trout and red fish. How to open oyster shells and fix crab gumbo...and chili...and popcorn...and make rafts out of old inner tubes and gunny sacks. I was continually amazed at his ability to do things like tie fragile mantles on the old Coleman lantern, keep a fire going in the rain, play the harmonica with his hands behind his back, and keep three strong-willed kids from tearing the house down.

Last night I realized I had him to thank for my deep love for America. And for knowing how to tenderly care for my wife. And for laughing at impossibilities. And for some of the habits I have picked up, like approaching people with a positive spirit rather than a negative one, staying with a task until it is finished, taking good care of my personal belongings, keeping my shoes shined, speaking up rather than mumbling, respecting authority, and standing alone (if necessary) in support of my personal convictions rather than giving in to more popular opinions. For these things I am deeply indebted to the man who raised me.

Certain smells and sounds now instantly remind me of my dad. Oyster stew. The ocean breeze. Smoke from an expensive cigar. The nostalgic whine of a harmonica. A camping lantern and white gas. Car polish. Fun songs from the 30s and 40s. Freshly mowed grass. A shrill whistle from a father to his kids around supper time. And Old Spice aftershave.

Because a father impacts his family so permanently, I think I understand better than ever what the Scripture means when Paul wrote:

> Having thus a fond affection for you, we were well-pleased to impart to you not only the gospel of God but also our own lives, because you had become very dear to us…just as you know how we were exhorting and encouraging and imploring each one of you as a father would his own children, so that you may walk in a manner worthy of the God who calls you into His own kingdom and glory (1 Thessalonians 2:8, 11–12).

Admittedly, much of my dad's instruction was indirect—by model rather than by explicit statement. I do not recall his overt declarations of love as clearly as I do his demonstrations of it. His life revolved around my mother, the darling and delight of his life. Of that I am sure. When she left over nine years ago, something of him died as well. And so—to her he has been joined and they are, together, with our Lord, in the closest possible companionship one can imagine.

In this my sister, my brother, and I find our greatest comfort—they are now forever *with the Lord*—eternally freed from pain and aging and death. Secure in Jesus Christ our Lord. Absent from the body and at home with Him. And with each other.

Last night I said goodbye. I'm still trying to believe it. You'd think it would be easy, since his illness had persisted for more than three years. How well I remember the Sunday he suffered that first in a series of strokes as I was preaching. God granted him several more years to teach many of us to appreciate the things we tend to take for granted.

He leaves in his legacy a well-marked Bible I treasure, a series of feelings that I need to deepen my roots, and a thousand memories that comfort me as I replace denial with acceptance and praise.

I await heaven's gate opening in the not-too-distant future. So do other Christians, who anxiously await Christ's return. Most of them anticipate hearing the soft strum of a harp or the sharp, staccato blast of a trumpet.

Not me. I will hear the nostalgic whine of a harmonica…held in the hands of the man who died last night…*or did he?* The memories are as fresh as this morning's sunrise.

JUST ENOUGH TIME

Barbara Baumgardner
from *Moody*, June 1991

Dad's heart is closing down. As I grasp this reality my own heart hurts deep within me.

Yet there's just enough life left for another day, another year, another Father's Day.

There's just enough life left to get his affairs in order; just enough time to teach Mom how to live alone.

There's just enough opportunity left for him to say, "I'm sorry, please forgive me before I go." Just enough strength to complete that last important project.

There's just enough time to say his goodbyes to us and prepare his hello to eternity.

And there's just enough time for me, too, to say, "Thank you, Dad, for caring for me so unselfishly. Thank you for insisting I grow up capable and independent, for caring about good health and good morals.

"Thank you for staying with Mom for almost 60 years, showing me that marriage can be good and permanent.

"Thank you for your discipline—even when I felt you were unjust, because it was then I learned patience and forgiveness.

"There's just enough time left to let you know I forgive you for your errors, and to ask you to forgive me for the times I blew it, trying your patience and betraying your expectations.

"There's just enough time to bake you one more loaf of the zucchini bread you love so much and watch your eyes light up as I slice it for you.

"And there might even be time enough for you to sharpen my kitchen knives once or twice more, because no one can put an edge on them like you do.

"And if there isn't enough time to share my overflowing heart, then I'll wait until we meet again. You know something, Dad? I believe that in our eternity, you and I are going to have just enough time to say and do and be everything we didn't have time for here.

"Happy Father's Day...I love you."

WHAT A HEART

What a teacher—what a giver—what a heart! He was all those old cliches. Big hearted. Tender hearted. He had a generous heart. He was all heart. It was the best used part he had and he just wore it out giving it to others. Now he will go on living in our hearts.

THE CHILDREN OF DICK WIMER

FROM HIS MEMORIAL SERVICE

A FATHER'S BLESSING

MORGAN CRYAR

FROM *DECISION* MAGAZINE

Many a morning as a child I stumbled through the darkness to our family's truck, fell back to sleep, then was awakened by the sound of the truck sputtering to a halt in the Louisiana woods. I can remember, even when I was too young to dress myself, climbing out of that truck alongside my dad—the most important person in my life at the time—and stepping into the gray, early morning light to hunt squirrels or deer.

One morning 10 years ago I was once again headed for the woods to hunt with Dad. But this time I was grown, with a family of my own. I had been touring for months and had promised to make a trip from our home in Nashville, Tennessee, to the swamps outside Lake Charles, Louisiana, where I had grown up. Though I didn't know it, this would be no ordinary morning. It was the morning that I would find out that Dad approved. This morning he would give me his blessing.

When we got into Dad's old truck and he turned the ignition key, music began to pour from a cassette in the tape deck. I knew the music well and was surprised to hear it in Dad's truck. It was my most recent recording, blaring into the morning stillness! I couldn't help myself; I said, "I didn't know you even had this. Do you listen to it?"

His answer amazed me. "It's the only thing I listen to." I glanced around, and sure enough, it was the only cassette in his truck. I was dumbstruck! He said, "This is my favorite," referring to the song playing at the time. I let his words sink in as he turned down the volume to match the morning.

We drove in silence down the road toward the hunting spot, and I wondered at what had just happened. It seems now like such a small thing—a few spoken words. But there seemed to be something different in the air. I sat taller in my seat. I looked at my dad out of the corner of my eye and thought back to two turning points in our relationship.

One turning point happened while I was in college. I remembered having it dawn on me that I had never heard my dad say that he loved me. I knew that he did, but I couldn't remember having heard him say so. That was something my dad just didn't do. For some reason it became important to me that I hear those words from his own lips. I knew, however, that he would never initiate it. So that summer, as I drove home from college, I determined to "force his hand" by telling him *first* that I loved him. Then he'd have to say it back. It would be simple. Just three little words. I anticipated a glorious new openness once I came home and said, "I love you, Dad," and then he would respond.

But simple is not always easy. The first day came and went, and I thought, "I *have* to tell him tomorrow!" The next day came and went. Then the next, and the next. Then 12 weeks passed, and it was the last day of my summer break. I was frustrated at not having said those three little words to my dad.

My little, beat-up car was packed and sitting on the gravel driveway. I promised myself that I would not start the engine until the deed was done. To someone with an emotionally open relationship with his own father, this may all seem a bit silly, but to me it was serious business. My palms were wet and my throat was dry. My knees grew weak as departure time came.

It had been a good summer visit. There was a general sadness in the house because I was headed back to school across the state. Finally I could wait no longer. I hugged my mom, my brother and my sister good-bye, and went back to find my dad.

I walked up to him, looked him in the eyes and said, "I love you, Dad."

He smiled a half smile, put his arms around me and said what I needed to hear: "I love you too, son." It seemed as though a thousand volts of electricity were in the air as we hugged each other (another thing that hasn't happened since I was a small child). It was such a little thing, but it changed everything!

From that point on, all of our conversations were signed off with: "I love you, Dad." "I love you too, son." It became commonplace to embrace when we greeted each other and when we parted. As plain as it sounds, it resulted in a new sweetness between my dad and me. The memory of it came back to me in the truck that morning on the way to the woods.

The other turning point came after college. I remembered that I had learned at a seminar about clearing my conscience with those whom I had wronged. This was entirely new to me—admitting guilt and receiving forgiveness from those I had offended.

Part of the process was to ask God to show me anyone and everyone with whom I needed to clear my conscience. Sure enough, at the top of the list was Dad.

So I sat down with my dad and started first with the worst things that I had done. I proceeded from there to the least serious offenses. I confessed everything that I knew had hurt him, even from my childhood. Then I simply asked, "Dad, will you forgive me?"

Just as I had expected, Dad was embarrassed and tried to shrug it off: "Aw, it's all right, son."

I said, "It will mean a lot to me if you will forgive me."

He looked right at me and said, "It has already been forgiven."

That was his way of saying that he had not held a grudge. And once again, everything changed. From that moment Dad treated me with new respect. I hadn't anticipated it, but he also began to treat me like an adult—like a friend.

In the stillness of the morning, on the way to the woods, these things floated through my memory, and I rested in my dad's approval of my calling, my work, my music.

I had no way of knowing just how precious his blessing would become to me. One short week later, after my family and I had driven back to Nashville, I received the telephone call from my brother, Tommy, telling me that Dad had walked out onto the porch and had died of a heart attack. He had been young and healthy—only 49 years old. It was my darkest day.

Though my family and I tasted intense grief, I still had much for which to be grateful. I had enjoyed 30 years with my dad—some of them as his friend. He had given me a strong enough start that I knew I could meet the challenge of rearing my own children, including my son who was born on Father's Day six years later.

Even though my dad is gone, in the wee hours of that morning on the way to the woods, he had given me something of great value to pass along—a father's blessing.

Do not follow where the path may lead.
Go instead where there is no path, and leave a trail.

ANONYMOUS

FAITH

WORRY

Some years ago someone gave my little boy a dollar. He brought it to me and said, "Daddy, keep this for me." But in a few minutes he came back and said, "Daddy, I'd better keep my own dollar." He tucked it in his pocket and went out to play. In a few minutes he came back with tears in his eyes, saying, "Daddy, I lost my dollar. Help me find it." How often we commit our burdens to the Lord and then fail to trust Him by taking matters into our own hands. Then, when we have messed things up, we pray, "Oh, Lord, help me, I'm in trouble."

The choice is yours. Do you want to trust your life in God's "pocket" or keep it in your own?

BILLY GRAHAM

FROM *UNTO THE HILLS*

A PERFECT MISTAKE

CHERYL WALTERMAN STEWART
FROM *LIVE*

Grandpa Nybakken loved life—especially when he could play a trick on somebody. At those times, his large Norwegian frame would shake with laughter while he feigned innocent surprise, exclaiming, "Oh, forevermore!" But on a cold Saturday in downtown Chicago, God played a trick on him, and Grandpa wasn't laughing.

Mother's father worked as a carpenter. On this particular day, he was building some crates for the clothes his church was sending to an orphanage in China. On his way home, he reached into his shirt pocket to find his glasses, but they were gone. He remembered putting them there that morning, so he drove back to the church. His search proved fruitless.

When he mentally replayed his earlier actions, he realized what happened: the glasses had slipped out of his pocket unnoticed and fallen into one of the crates, which he had nailed shut. His brand new glasses were heading for China!

The Great Depression was at its height and Grandpa had six children. He had spent $20 for those glasses that very morning. He was upset by the thought of having to buy another pair.

"It's not fair," he told God as he drove home in frustration. "I've been very faithful in giving of my time and money to your work, and now this."

Several months later the director of the orphanage was on furlough in the United States. He wanted to visit all the churches that supported him in China, so he came to speak one Sunday night at my grandfather's small church in Chicago. Grandpa and his family sat in their customary seats among the sparse congregation.

The missionary began by thanking the people for their faithfulness in supporting the orphanage.

"But most of all," he said, "I must thank you for the glasses you sent last year. You see, the Communists had just swept through the orphanage, destroying everything, including my glasses. I was desperate.

"Even if I had the money, there was simply no way of replacing those glasses. Along with not being able to see well, I experienced headaches every day, so my coworkers and I were much in prayer about this. Then your crates arrived. When my staff removed the covers, they found a pair of glasses lying on top."

The missionary paused long enough to let his words sink in. Then, still gripped with the wonder of it all, he continued: "Folks, when I tried on the glasses, it was as though they had been custom-made just for me! I want to thank you for being a part of that."

The people listened, happy for the miraculous glasses. But the missionary surely must have confused their church with another, they thought. There were no glasses on their list of items to be sent overseas.

But sitting quietly in the back, with tears streaming down his face, an ordinary carpenter realized the Master Carpenter had used him in an extraordinary way.

WHEN GOD TAKES YOUR HAND

RON MEHL

CONDENSED FROM *GOD WORKS THE NIGHT SHIFT*

Little feet aren't the only ones that stumble. One of my friends recently became a grandfather for the first time. Ask any new grandparent what their grandchild looks like and, without a doubt, they'll either unravel an accordion wallet with a six-foot string of pictures or simply brag about the child for hours.

One day I was visiting this friend while he was charged with watching his granddaughter. "Watch this, Ron," he said as he swept the little girl into his arms. He stood her up against the couch. Even with her back against it, I could see it was all she could do to stay in a standing position.

Then he said, "Come to Bumpa, darlin', come to ol' Bumpa!"

The fat spongy little legs that would barely support her while leaning against the couch absolutely wouldn't support her in the big world on her own. She took one short, tiny step, and fell into a pile of legs, diaper, and corn-silk curls. Then she just grinned.

Grandpa smiled, too, but seemed a little embarrassed. He stood her up against the couch for another try.

"Come on little darlin'. Come see ol' Bumpa. Come on, sweetheart!"

Her heart was in it. Her spirit was game. Out she stepped. Down she went.

My friend laughed again but this time was not quite able to conceal a growing fear that he might have bragged about this child's mobile abilities a tad early.

"Maybe she's just had a long day, Bumpa," I teased.

He smirked. One more try. One more pile of 10-month-old on the floor. This landing was a little harder than before, and the toddler began to whimper. My friend reached for the standard excuse.

"Aw, well, she's just tired. Too tired from all that walking she did yesterday."

Then he did what I thought was a wonderful thing. Instead of just leaving the little lady to crawl off defeated on her own, he wanted her to be encouraged by her efforts. He reached down with his big work-hardened hands, took hold of her chubby little fingers, lifted her up, turned her around, and set her feet on top of his. When he lifted his left foot, her left foot went up. Same with the right foot. They walked around the room with a precision that would have made a Marine drill sergeant proud. An expression of assurance and delight dawned on that little girl's face. She was walking! She'd been instantly transformed from a stumbling toddler to a little woman striding the runway in a Miss America pageant. All because of Bumpa's helpful hands and feet.

She laughed with pleasure and walked with pride, too young to realize that her little feet balanced on big feet that had walked many miles, that her little hands clung to big hands that had carried heavy loads, that her equilibrium depended on the balance of a man who'd marched in mud, walked on ice, and navigated fast-moving streams in hipwaders. And all the while she was cheered along by a grandfather's heart that anticipated her needs and loved her very much.

As children of a heavenly Father, we too need help getting around in life. David had the right idea when he wrote: "Your right hand has held me up, Your gentleness has made me great. You enlarged my path under me, and my feet did not slip" (Psalm 18:35–36).

The heavenly Father takes our hands in his. He lifts us gently. He holds us up. He smoothes the path ahead. He keeps us from blundering off the path. Will we still stumble and lose our balance at times? Sure. But

Scripture assures us that if we're clinging to his hand, our stumbles will not result in devastating falls. "The steps of a good man are ordered by the LORD, And He delights in his way. Though he fall, he shall not utterly be cast down: For the LORD upholds him with His hand" (Psalm 37:23–24).

PLANNING AHEAD

Years ago, a minister waited in line to have his car filled with gas just before a long holiday weekend. The attendant worked quickly, but there were many cars ahead of him in front of the service station. Finally, the attendant motioned him toward a vacant pump.

"Reverend," said the young man, "sorry about the delay. It seems as if everyone waits until the last minute to get ready for a long trip." The minister chuckled, "I know what you mean. It's the same in my business."

KENNETH BOA

FROM *THAT I MAY KNOW GOD*

PEACE

BILLY GRAHAM

FROM *UNTO THE HILLS*

The sea was beating against the rocks in huge, dashing waves. The lightning was flashing, the thunder was roaring, the wind was blowing; but the little bird was asleep in the crevice of the rock, its head serenely under its wing, sound asleep.

That is peace—to be able to sleep in the storm! In Christ, we are relaxed and at peace in the midst of the confusions, bewilderments, and perplexities of this life. The storm rages, but our hearts are at rest. We have found peace—at last!

THE OAK TREE

MAX LUCADO

FROM *NO WONDER THEY CALL HIM THE SAVIOR*

In a recent trip to my hometown I took some time to go see a tree. "A live oak tree," my dad had called it (with the accent on "live"). It was nothing more than a sapling, so thin I could wrap my hand around it and touch my middle finger to my thumb. The West Texas wind scattered the fall leaves and caused me to zip up my coat. There is nothing colder than a prairie wind, especially in a cemetery.

"A special tree," I said to myself, "with a special job." I looked around. The cemetery was lined with elms but no oaks. The ground was dotted with tombstones but no trees. Just this one. A special tree for a special man.

About three years ago Daddy began noticing a steady weakening of his muscles. It began in his hands. He then felt it in his calves. Next his arms thinned a bit.

He mentioned his condition to my brother-in-law, who is a physician. My brother-in-law, alarmed, sent him to a specialist. The specialist conducted a lengthy battery of tests—blood, neurological, and muscular—and he reached his conclusion. Lou Gehrig's disease. A devastating crippler. No one knows the cause or the cure. The only sure thing about it is its cruelty and accuracy.

I looked down at the plot of ground that would someday entomb my father. Daddy always wanted to be buried under an oak tree so he bought this one. "Special order from the valley," he had boasted. "Had to get special permission from the city council to put it here." (That wasn't hard in this dusty oil field town where everybody knows everybody.)

The lump got tighter in my throat. A lesser man might have been angry. Another man might have given up. But Daddy didn't. He knew that his days were numbered so he began to get his house in order.

The tree was only one of the preparations he made. He improved the house for Mom by installing a sprinkler system and a garage door opener and by painting the trim. He got the will updated. He verified the insurance and retirement policies. He bought some stock to go toward his grandchildren's education. He planned his funeral. He bought cemetery plots for himself and Mom. He prepared his kids through words of assurance and letters of love. And last of all, he bought the tree. A live oak tree. (Pronounced with an accent on "live.")

Final acts. Final hours. Final words.

They reflect a life well lived. So do the last words of our Master. When on the edge of death, Jesus, too, got his house in order:

A final prayer of forgiveness.

A plea honored.

A request of love.

A question of suffering.

A confession of humanity.

A call of deliverance.

A cry of completion.

Words of chance muttered by a desperate martyr? No. Words of intent, painted by the Divine Deliverer on the canvas of sacrifice.

Final words. Final acts. Each one is a window through which the cross can be better understood. Each one opens a treasury of promises. "So that is where you learned it," I said aloud as though speaking to my father. I smiled to myself and thought, "It's much easier to die like Jesus if you have lived like him for a lifetime."

The final hours are passing now. The gentle flame on his candle grows weaker and weaker. He lies in peace. His body dying, his spirit living. No longer can he get out of bed. He has chosen to live his last days at home. It won't be long. Death's windy draft will soon exhaust the flickering candle and it will be over.

I looked one last time at the slender oak. I touched it as if it had been hearing my thoughts. "Grow," I whispered. "Grow strong. Stand tall. Yours is a valued treasure."

As I drove home through the ragged oil field patchwork, I kept thinking about that tree. Though feeble, the decades will find it strong. Though slender, the years will add thickness and strength. Its last years will be its best. Just like my father's. Just like my Master's. "It is much easier to die like Jesus if you have lived like him for a lifetime."

"Grow, young tree." My eyes were misting. "Stand strong. Yours is a valued treasure."

He was awake when I got home. I leaned over his bed. "I checked on the tree," I told him. "It's growing."

He smiled.

DON'T GIVE UP

MORRIS CHALFANT
FROM *THE ADVOCATE*

There is a painting that shows the devil at a chessboard with a young man. The devil has just made his move, and the young man's queen is checkmated. On his face is written defeat and despair. One day the great chess genius Paul Morphy stood looking at that painting. He studied carefully the position on the board. Suddenly his face lit up and he shouted to the young man in the painting, "You still have a move—don't give up, you still have a move!"

We come to those moments when it seems we are checkmated. We see no winning move we can make. Then the great Master of all life comes closer to us. He remembers one day when He prayed to be spared from the cross: "Let this cup pass from me," he pleaded. The cross seemed the end of His world. But there was yet another move. Beyond the cross was an empty tomb—and victory.

That same Christ can see beyond your cross to some triumph. "Don't give up, you still have a move," He says.

JUST A KID
WITH CEREBRAL PALSY

TONY CAMPOLO

FROM *U*, APRIL/MAY 1998

I was asked to be a counselor in a junior high camp. Everybody ought
to be a counselor in a junior high camp—just once. A junior high kid's
concept of a good time is picking on people. And in this particular case,
at this particular camp, there was a little boy who was suffering from cerebral palsy. His name was Billy. And they picked on him.

Oh, they picked on him. As he walked across the camp with his
uncoordinated body they would line up and imitate his grotesque move-
ments. I watched him one day as he was asking for direction.
"Which...way is...the...craft...shop?" he stammered, his mouth contort-
ing. And the boys mimicked in that same awful stammer, "It's...over...
there...Billy." And then they laughed at him. I was irate.

But my furor reached its highest pitch when on Thursday morning it
was Billy's cabin's turn to give devotions. I wondered what would happen,
because they had appointed Billy to be the speaker. I knew that they just
wanted to get him up there to make fun of him. As he dragged his way to
the front, you could hear the giggles rolling over the crowd. It took little
Billy almost five minutes to say seven words.

"Jesus...loves...me...and...I...love...Jesus."

When he finished, there was dead silence. I looked over my shoulder and saw junior high boys bawling all over the place. A revival broke out in that camp after Billy's short testimony. And as I travel all over the world, I find missionaries and preachers who say, "Remember me? I was converted at that junior high camp." We counselors had tried everything to get those kids interested in Jesus. We even imported baseball players whose batting averages had gone up since they had started praying. But God chose not to use the superstars. He chose a kid with cerebral palsy to break the spirits of the haughty. He's that kind of God.

Sin will take you further than you ever intended to stray
Sin will keep you longer than you ever intended to stay
Sin will cost you more than you ever intended to pay.
ANOYMOUS

EVEN IF IT'S DARK

RON MEHL

FROM *GOD WORKS THE NIGHT SHIFT*

He was a strong man facing an enemy beyond his strength.

His young wife had become gravely ill, then suddenly passed away, leaving the big man alone with a wide-eyed, flaxen-haired girl, not quite five years old.

The service in the village chapel was simple, and heavy with grief. After the burial at the small cemetery, the man's neighbors gathered around him. "Please, bring your little girl and stay with us for several days," someone said. "You shouldn't go back home just yet."

Broken-hearted though he was, the man answered, "Thank you, friends, for the kind offer. But we need to go back home—where she was. My baby and I must face this."

So they returned, the big man and his little girl, to what now seemed an empty, lifeless house. The man brought his daughter's little bed into his room, so they could face the first dark night together.

As the minutes slipped by that night, the young girl was having a dreadful time trying to sleep…and so was her father. What could pierce a man's heart deeper than a child sobbing for a mother who would never come back?

Long into the night the little one continued to weep. The big man reached down into her bed and tried to comfort her as best he could. After a while, the little girl managed to stop crying—but only out of sorrow for her father. Thinking his daughter was asleep, the father looked up and said brokenly, "I trust You, Father, but…it's as dark as midnight!"

Hearing her dad's prayer, the little girl began to cry again.

"I thought you were asleep, baby," he said.

"Papa, I did try. I was sorry for you. I did try. But—I couldn't go to sleep. Papa, did you ever know it could be so dark? Why Papa? I can't even see you, it's so dark." Then, through her tears, the little girl whispered, "But you love me even if it's dark—don't you, Papa? You love me even if I don't see you, don't you, Papa?"

For an answer, the big man reached across with his massive hands, lifted his little girl out of her bed, brought her over onto his chest, and held her, until at last she fell asleep.

When she was finally quiet, he began to pray. He took his little daughter's cry to him, and passed it up to God.

"Father, it's dark as midnight. I can't see You at all. But You love me, even when it's dark and I can't see, don't You?"

TRAVELING THROUGH

BILLY GRAHAM

FROM *HOPE FOR THE TROUBLED HEART*

My father-in-law, Nelson Bell, held on to the things of this world so loosely that when he died and we opened his closet, there were only two suits hanging there. Things were not that important to him.

In my travels I have found that those who keep Heaven in view remain serene and cheerful in the darkest day. If the glories of Heaven were more real to us, if we lived less for material things and more for things eternal and spiritual, we would be less easily disturbed by this present life.

A friend told me about stopping on a street corner in London and listening to a man play the bagpipes. He was playing "Amazing Grace" and smiling from ear to ear. My friend asked him if he was from Scotland, and he answered, "No sir, my home is in Heaven. I'm just traveling through this world."

TOMMY'S DADDIES

CASANDRA LINDELL

I t had been a hot, tiring day at the outdoor music festival. Four-year-
old Tommy sat in my lap with his head resting against my chest. His
mother had taken his brother to find a drink of water. His father was packing up the display booth. Tommy and I went to find a quiet place on the
stairs behind a building. He was sleepy and cuddly, and his droopy eyes
looked at the stars.

"How did the stars get up there?" he asked.

"God put them there."

"My dad told me that. But God died." Tommy sounded very sad but
I had to smile.

"Yes, he did. And then he came back to life again."

"Oh yeah. I always forget that part." He was very serious as he studied the night sky.

Then he asked where his dad was. I said he was putting things in
boxes to take to the car.

"I miss him," he told me. Tommy wasn't speaking as a child whose
father was never around. I knew these friends well, and his dad spent lots
of time with his boys—laughing, loving, and teaching. His influence was
easy to see. Little Tommy missed his dad because he was so used to being
with him.

So Tommy and I sat, looking at the stars. We talked about being lonely.

"But you know," I said, "even when your daddy and mommy aren't here, God is always here."

Tommy was quiet. I thought for just a moment that he may have fallen asleep. Then, very softly and still looking at the sky, he said, "If God was my daddy, I'd have the best daddy in the whole world."

Again, I smiled. "He is your father, Tommy. He's the Father in heaven who loves you very much—even more than your daddy does, and he promises he'll never leave you."

"Oh yeah," Tommy said. "I forgot that part too."

As he finally drifted off to sleep, I sat looking at the stars alone. I thought about two fathers—both of them the best daddies a boy could have—laughing, loving, and teaching. Their influence was indeed easy to see.

LEARNING 'BOUT PRAYER

HOWARD HENDRICKS

FROM *STANDING TOGETHER*

He came to know the Lord on a Thursday evening, and on Sunday he showed up at church. The pastor announced that we were going to have an evening service, and of course the guy didn't know enough to stay home. So he showed up again. That's when he learned that our church had a Bible study and prayer meeting on Wednesday night, so he came that evening as well.

I sat next to him at the prayer meeting, and just before we got started, he turned to me and asked, "Do you think they'd mind if I prayed?"

"Of course not," I reassured him. "That's what we're here for."

"Yeah, I know," he said, "but I've got a problem. I can't pray the way you people do."

I told him, "That's no problem, friend. You should thank God for that!"

Well, we started praying, and I could tell he was too nervous to take part. Finally, I put my hand on his thigh to encourage him. I'll never forget his prayer: "Lord, this is Jim," he began. "I'm the one who met you last Thursday night. I'm sorry, Lord, because I can't say it the way the rest of these people do, but I want to tell you the best I know how. I love you, Lord. I really do. Thanks a lot. I'll see you later."

I tell you, that prayer ignited our prayer meeting! Some of us had been doing a good job of talking about theology in prayer—you know, exploring the universe of doctrine, scraping the Milky Way with our big words. But this guy prayed—earnestly!

My children have taught me many things about theology. When they were quite young, we had a scholar visiting our home. After our meal, we were ready for our customary time of family worship, and we invited the man to join us. When it came time to pray, the kids, in typical childlike fashion, thanked Jesus for the tricycle and the sandbox and the fence and so on. Our guest could scarcely wait to take me aside.

"Professor Hendricks," he began, very much the lecturer that he was, "you don't mean to tell me that you're a professor in a theological seminary, and yet you teach your children to pray for things like that?"

"I certainly do," I replied. "Do you ever pray about your Ford?" I knew he did. He had to: he was riding mostly on faith and frayed fabric!

"Of course," he replied, "but that's different."

"Oh, really?" I countered. "What makes you think your Ford is more important to God than my boy's tricycle?" Then I pressed him further. "You're on the road a lot. Do you ever pray for protection?"

"Brother Hendricks, I never go anywhere but that I pray for the Lord's journeying mercies."

"Well, safety is essentially what my boy is thanking Jesus for when he thanks him for the fence. That fence keeps out those great big dogs on the other side!"

TWO PRAYERS

ANDREW GILLIES

FROM *MASTERPIECE OF RELIGIOUS VERSE*

Last night my little boy confessed to me
Some childish wrong;
And kneeling at my knee,
He prayed with tears—
"Dear God, make me a man
Like Daddy—wise and strong;
I know You can."

Then while he slept
I knelt beside his bed,
Confessed my sins,
And prayed with low-bowed head.
"O God, make me a child
Like my child here—
Pure, guileless
Trusting Thee with faith sincere."

THE BOOTBLACK AND THE PH.D.

RUTH GRAHAM

FROM *LEGACY OF A PACK RAT*

The small bootblack polished away with enthusiasm. He liked his work—turning a pair of scruffy leather shoes into a shining work of art.

He liked the men who called him by name, sat in his chair, and buried their noses in the morning newspaper.

He especially liked the little foreign man with the funny accent.

His friendly, "Today, how you are?" let him know this man really cared how he was. What the bootblack did not know was that the man with the funny accent was from Soviet Georgia and held three earned doctoral degrees. He just kept polishing away happily.

The day came when the unhappy Ph.D. could stand it no longer. Looking down at the bootblack working so cheerfully and enthusiastically on his shoes, and thinking on his own inner misery, he put down his paper.

"Why always you so happy?" he asked.

Surprised, the bootblack paused in his polishing, sat back on his heels, scratched his head thoughtfully for a moment, then said simply, "Jesus. He loves me. He died so God could forgive my badness. He makes me happy."

The newspaper snapped up around the face of the professor, and the bootblack went back to polishing his shoes.

But the brilliant University of Pennsylvania professor could not escape those simple words. They were what brought him eventually to the Savior.

Years later, my husband's college major was anthropology. His beloved and admired professor was the renowned Dr. Alexander Grigolia of the University of Pennsylvania, who found God through the simple testimony of a bootblack those many years before.

GREATNESS

When Jesus gathered His disciples for the Last Supper they were having trouble over which one was the greatest. Gathered at the Passover feast, the disciples were keenly aware that someone needed to wash the others' feet. The problem was that the only people who washed feet were the least. So there they sat, feet caked with dirt. It was such a sore point that they were not even going to talk about it. No one wanted to be considered the least. Then Jesus took a towel and a basin and so redefined greatness.

RICHARD FOSTER

THINKING OF LIFE

DAVID R. JOHNSON
FROM *THE LIGHT BEHIND THE STAR*

I told Maggie I would be gone about an hour, then left to complete some errands. When I returned, she and the girls came out to meet me as I got out of the car. Maggie asked if I had been listening to the news, and I told her no. She said a new bulletin on TV reported that two San Jose police officers had been shot—one was killed instantly and the other was listed in critical condition. She said no details were given of the shooting, and the two officers weren't named.

I felt the hot flash of adrenaline shoot through my body as I hurried inside and grabbed the telephone. I had trouble remembering what the phone number was for the main police desk, then became frustrated when I received a busy signal. I continued dialing until I finally reached an officer manning the phones. After I identified myself, I asked what had happened.

He told me the two men's names and gave some details of the shooting. I felt the strength leave my body as the realization sank in: A fellow officer and friend had been killed, and another was critically wounded.

"What type of blood do you have?" the desk official asked. "They need blood for transfusions during the operation."

I didn't have the right type that was needed. I hung up the phone, feeling a sense of helplessness.

The news media broadcast the appeal for blood for the injured officer, and soon lines of cars were parked outside the hospital as concerned
citizens and officers from other agencies came to donate their blood.

I stayed by the radio and television set the rest of the afternoon, listening for information. On the televised six o'clock news, as a broadcaster
described the shooting scene and the events that led up to it, I watched
footage taken at the scene earlier in the day. My heart raced as the camera
focused on a yellow blanket covering the slain officer's body. Beneath the
blanket was the unmistakable white stripe running the length of our uniform's pants. From one side of the blanket, an arm protruded, lying
motionless on the ground. This wasn't Hollywood; this was real life—and
death.

The picture changed to a live broadcast outside the hospital where
the other officer had been taken. The news announcer said word had just
been received that the other officer had died while in surgery.

I felt as if I were in a dream, and I was anxious to wake up so I could
see that all this was unreal. But in my heart I knew it was no dream. Two
police officers were dead. They weren't the first officers to die in the line
of duty in San Jose, and I knew in my heart they wouldn't be the last. But
this was the first time the department had lost two officers at once, and
the violent way in which it happened brought a feeling of shock to the
entire city.

I looked across at Maggie and the girls, and wondered if being a
police officer was worth the risk that was present each time I walked out
the front door of our home on my way to work. Was it fair to them for me
to take those risks that go with pinning a star over my heart and carrying
a gun at my side? Wasn't my nineteen years as a police officer long enough
to have taken such risks? Maybe the people who had said to me over the
years that they wouldn't do my job for a million dollars were right. Maybe
the price of being a cop *was* too high.

But if so, who would be cops? Who would be there to answer the
calls for help when the assailant attacks or the lost child needs to be
found? Who would make it safe to drive the highways or walk the streets?
Who would be willing to stand between the criminal and the law-abiding
citizen? If not me, who?

I knew I couldn't expect anyone else to be a cop if I were unwilling—

especially since I knew that being a policeman was what God wanted me to be.

And I knew I could rest in the wisdom of His will.

Six days later, the funeral for the two officers was held. Only a few months earlier I had been in the honor guard for the last San Jose officer to die in the line of duty—in a motorcycle accident—and I was asked to be in this one too. I could still remember the pain of loss I felt during the first funeral. And now, I again stood at attention in my dress uniform, in front of the same large church. But this time there were *two* flag-draped coffins that held the bodies of fellow officers gunned down in the streets that they had sworn to defend. Two officers who had gotten up that morning thinking it would be just another day for them, doing the same job they had done for years. Another day assisting people when they called for help. Another day of taking reports and perhaps writing tickets. Another day to maybe laugh along with the other officers during the morning briefing session. Neither of them thought their day would end in a hail of gunfire that would leave them dead.

As we followed the coffins into the auditorium, I thought about my early morning routine on workdays: Bible study and prayer time; packing my lunch, and slipping into the lunchbox the note that my daughter writes me everyday; kissing Maggie goodbye as I walk out the door; and flashing my car's lights three times as an "I love you" sign, as I wave and drive away. I rarely if ever think that I might not be coming home that evening...

It took nearly thirty minutes for the 4,500 police officers from more than two hundred agencies throughout California to file into the church. Some stood in the halls, while others stood outside and listened to the service on loud-speakers.

The police chaplain gave a fitting message for the two officers. Then an officer got up and gave a eulogy to his fallen friend. When he sat down, an officer's wife stepped in front and began singing:

> When peace like a river attendeth my way,
> when sorrows like sea billows roll;
> whatever my lot, Thou has taught me to say,
> "It is well, it is well with my soul."

As I stood soaking in the words to one of my favorite hymns, I knew that it was truly well with my soul. The pain of loss would stay for a long time, the memories would continue, and questions about the tragedy would go unanswered—but God would still be in control, always and forever.

The service ended and the thousands of officers filed past the coffins. Many stopped and gave a farewell salute to their fallen comrades, then waited outside the church as the coffins were brought out for the last time. As part of the honor guard I helped fold the flags to be given to our police chief, who then presented them to the officers' families.

As the sound of the twenty-one gun salute faded away, taps were played. The notes echoed off of the surrounding hills as if a distant bugler were returning the tribute to the dead. Again I remembered giving this goodbye to a fellow officer only months before: the Scriptures had been read, the songs had been sung, the salutes had been given, the guns had been sounded, the folded flag had been presented. And taps had been played.

Now again, the last tears fell to the ground and clung to the grass like morning dew. I stood in silence and thought about death. I found that the thought drew me closer to Jesus, the Giver and Keeper of life.

And the words echoed within: "It is well with my soul."

Jesus was born into the family of men
that we might be Born Again into the family of God.

RIGHT ON TIME

RON MEHL

FROM *SURPRISE ENDINGS*

Roger Simms had just left the military and was anxious to take his uniform off once and for all. He was hitchhiking home, and his heavy duffel bag made the trip even more arduous than hitchhiking normally is. Flashing his thumb to an oncoming car, he lost hope when he saw that it was a shiny, black, expensive car, so new that it had a temporary license in the back window…hardly the type of car that would stop for a hitchhiker.

But to his amazement, the car stopped and the passenger door opened. He ran toward the car, placed his duffel carefully in the back, and slid into the leather-covered front seat. He was greeted by the friendly smile of a handsome older gentleman with distinguished gray hair and a deep tan.

"Hello, son. Are you on leave or are you going home for good?"

"I just got out of the army, and I'm going home for the first time in several years," answered Roger.

"Well, you're in luck if you're going to Chicago," smiled the man.

"Not quite that far," said Roger, "but my home is on the way. Do you live there, Mister?"

"Hanover. Yes, I have a business there." And with that, they were on their way.

After giving each other brief life histories, and talking about everything under the sun, Roger (who was a Christian) felt a strong compulsion to witness to Mr. Hanover about Christ. But witnessing to an elderly, wealthy businessman who obviously had everything he could ever want was a scary prospect indeed. Roger kept putting it off, but as he neared his destination, he realized that it was now or never.

"Mr. Hanover," began Roger, "I would like to talk to you about something very important." He then proceeded to explain the way of salvation, ultimately asking Mr. Hanover if he would like to receive Christ as his Savior. To Roger's astonishment, the big car pulled over to the side of the road; Roger thought for a moment that Mr. Hanover was about to throw him out. Then a strange and wonderful thing happened: the businessman bowed his head to the steering wheel and began to cry, affirming that he did in fact want to accept Christ into his heart. He thanked Roger for talking to him, saying that, "This is the greatest thing that has ever happened to me." He then dropped Roger at his house and traveled on toward Chicago.

Five years went by, and Roger Simms married, had a child, and started a business of his own. One day, while packing for a business trip to Chicago, he came across a small, gold-embossed business card which Mr. Hanover had given him years earlier.

When Roger arrived in Chicago, he looked up Hanover Enterprises, and found it to be located downtown in a very tall and important-looking building. The receptionist told him that it would be impossible to see Mr. Hanover, but that if he was an old friend, he would be able to see Mrs. Hanover. A little disappointed, he was led into a poshly-decorated office where a woman in her fifties was sitting at a huge oak desk.

She extended her hand. "You knew my husband?"

Roger explained how Mr. Hanover had been kind enough to give him a ride back home.

A look of interest passed across her face. "Can you tell me what date that was?"

"Sure," said Roger. "It was May 7th, five years ago, the day I was discharged from the army."

"And did anything special happen on your ride…anything unusual?"

Roger hesitated. Should he mention giving his witness? Had it been some source of contention between the two, which resulted in a marital breakup or separation? But once again, he felt the prompting of the Lord to be truthful. "Mrs. Hanover, your husband accepted the Lord into his heart that day. I explained the gospel message to him, and he pulled to the side of the road and wept, and then chose to pray a prayer of salvation."

Suddenly, she began to sob uncontrollably. After several minutes, she regained enough control to explain what had happened: "I grew up in a Christian home, but my husband did not. I had prayed for my husband's salvation for many years, and I believed God would save him. But just after he let you out of his car, on May 7th, he passed away in a horrible head-on collision. He never arrived home. I thought God had not kept His promise, and I stopped living for the Lord five years ago because I blamed Him for not keeping His word."

I can identify with Mrs. Hanover. Perhaps you can, too. There are long, lonely stretches in life when it seems as if God has simply become indifferent toward our plight and bored or apathetic about our fervent prayers.

It's like staring at tightly wrapped, mysterious, and unavailable presents under a tree. As time goes on and hope stretches thin, we begin to wonder if God really has any gifts for us.

Maybe you've been waiting a long time for situations to change in your life. You've been waiting for a change in your health, in your relationships, in your spouse, in your children, in your job, in your finances, in your spiritual life. And it seems the delay goes on forever. It seems Christmas will never come. It seems the light will never change. It seems you've dialed the Lord's 9-1-1 line a thousand times and He's never answered.

Mary and Martha know all about that. They watched their brother weaken and fail. His life slipped though their fingers like sand and they couldn't stop it and the Lord didn't come.

But then He did come. And it was too late. But it wasn't too late. Because what He had in mind was something so far beyond their thoughts and experience and hopes and dreams that they didn't even think to ask for it.

It was a Very Good Thing wrapped in a Very Bad Thing.

And He delivered it Himself...right on time.

He always does.

THE FINAL GLANCE

MAX LUCADO

FROM *SIX HOURS, ONE FRIDAY*

Max, your dad's awake."

I had been watching a movie on television. One of those thrillers that takes you from the here and now and transports you to the somewhere and sometime. My mother's statement seemed to come from another world. The real world.

I turned toward my father. He was looking at me.

His head was all he could turn. Lou Gehrig's disease had leeched his movement, taking from him everything but his faith...and his eyes.

It was his eyes that called me to walk over to his bedside. I had been home for almost two weeks, on special leave from Brazil, due to his worsening condition. He had slept most of the last few days, awakening only when my mother would bathe him or clean his sheets.

Next to his bed was a respirator—a metronome of mortality that pushed air into his lungs through a hole in his throat. The bones in his hand protruded like spokes in an umbrella. His fingers, once firm and strong, were curled and lifeless. I sat on the edge of his bed and ran my hands over his barreled rib cage. I put my hand on his forehead. It was hot...hot and damp. I stroked his hair.

"What is it, Dad?"

He wanted to say something. His eyes yearned. His eyes refused to release me. If I looked away for a moment, they followed me, and were still looking when I looked back.

"What is it?"

I'd seen that expression before. I was seven years old, eight at the most. Standing on the edge of a diving board for the first time, wondering if I would survive the plunge. The board dipped under my seventy pounds. I looked behind me at the kids who were pestering me to hurry up and jump. I wondered what they would do if I asked them to move over so I could get down. Tar and feather me, I supposed.

So caught between ridicule and a jump into certain death, I did the only thing I knew to do—I shivered.

Then I heard him, "It's all right, son, come on in." I looked down. My father had dived in. He was treading water awaiting my jump. Even as I write, I can see his expression—tanned face, wet hair, broad smile, and bright eyes. His eyes were assuring and earnest. Had he not said a word, they would have conveyed the message. But he did speak. "Jump, it's all right."

So I jumped.

Twenty-three years later the tan was gone, the hair thin and the face drawn. But the eyes hadn't changed. They were bold. And their message hadn't changed. I knew what he was saying. Somehow he knew I was afraid. Somehow he perceived that I was shivering as I looked into the deep. And somehow, he, the dying, had the strength to comfort me, the living.

I placed my cheek in the hollow of his. My tears dripped on his hot face. I said softly what his throat wanted to, but couldn't. "It's all right," I whispered. "It's going to be all right."

When I raised my head, his eyes were closed. I would never see them open again.

He left me with a final look. One last statement of the eyes. One farewell message from the captain before the boat would turn out to sea. One concluding assurance from a father to a son, "It's all right."

I hope these stories have touched your heart
and encouraged your soul. If you wish to reprint any of
the stories, please check the following pages and write directly
to the source where the story was first published.

For other information write to

Multnomah Publishers
Post Office Box 1720
Sisters, Oregon 97759

The LORD bless you and keep you;
the LORD make his face shine upon you
and be gracious to you;
the LORD turn his face toward you
and give you peace.

NUMBERS 6:24–27

STORIES FOR A WOMAN'S HEART
Coming February 1999! In the same tender, uplifting, and heartwarming style of *Stories for the Heart,* this wonderful collection of stories honors mothers. Some of our most-loved authors—Ruth Graham, Gigi Tchividjian, Kay James, Luci Swindoll, and others—share moving stories about how their mothers instilled Christian values and virtues into their lives.

☞ Perfect for any woman on Mother's Day, her birthday, or Christmas.

ISBN 1-57673-474-9 | $11.99

OTHER QUALITY RELEASES

STORIES FOR THE FAMILY'S HEART
Stories for the Family's Heart continues in the tradition of the Stories for the Heart series—tender tales that deliver Christian values in a captivating and wondrous way that appeals to parents, grandparents, and children.

ISBN 1-57673-472-2 | $11.99

CHRISTMAS STORIES FOR THE HEART
Christmas Stories for the Heart invites readers to curl up by the fire and warm their souls with these classic stories. This heartwarming, tender, and uplifting treasury is the perfect gift! Includes favorite Christmas stories by Max Lucado, Billy Graham, Charles Swindoll, Joni Eareckson Tada, and more! This wonderful collection will renew your faith, hope, and love for holiday seasons.

ISBN 1-57673-456-0 | $9.99

AVAILABLE NOW, THE BOOKS THAT BEGAN A HEARTFELT TRADITION

STORIES FOR THE HEART

OVER ONE MILLION IN PRINT

Good stories endure the passage of the years, and this treasury of timeless tales—written by today's best Christian communicators—offers a wealth of encouragement, compassion, and love destined to minister to multiple generations.

✔ Stories by Max Lucado, James Dobson, Kay Arthur, Billy Graham, Chuck Swindoll, Paul Harvey, and many others.

ISBN 1-57673-127-8 | $11.99

AND THE TREASURED SEQUEL

MORE STORIES FOR THE HEART

OVER 300,000 SOLD

A sequel to *Stories for the Heart*, *More Stories for the Heart* offers more than one hundred stories that will hug readers' hearts and encourage their souls.

ISBN 1-57673-142-1 | $11.99

NOTES

More than a thousand books and magazines were researched for this collection as well as reviewing hundreds of stories sent by friends and readers of the *Stories for the Heart* collection. A diligent search has been made to trace original ownership, and when necessary, permission to reprint has been obtained. If I have overlooked giving proper credit to anyone, please accept my apologies. If you will contact Multnomah Publishers, Inc., Post Office Box 1720, Sisters, Oregon 97759, corrections will be made prior to additional printings.

Notes and acknowledgements are listed by story title in the order they appear in each section of the book. For permission to reprint any of the stories please request permission from the original source listed in the following bibliography. Grateful acknowledgement is made to authors, publishers, and agents who granted permission for reprinting these stories.

VIRTUE

"The Student's Mite" by David R. Collins, freelance writer, Moline, IL. Used by permission. Quoted from *Teachers in Focus* magazine, December/January 1996–1997.

"By the Way, My Name Is Joe" author unknown.

"Lessons From a Wallet" by Bruce McIver from *Stories I Couldn't Tell While I Was a Pastor,* Bruce McIver, copyright © 1991 (Word Publishing, Nashville, TN). All rights reserved.

"Getting Rid of Things" from *Home Town Tales* by Philip Gulley (Multnomah Publishers, Inc., Sisters, OR, © 1998). Used by permission.

"Arthur Berry's Answer" by Dale Galloway, Director of 20/20 Vision, quoted from *How to Feel Like a Somebody Again* (Harvest House Publishers, Eugene, OR, © 1978). Used by permission of the author.

"It's a Start" from *Leaving the Light On/Home Remedies* by Gary Smalley and John Trent (Multnomah Publishers, Inc., Sisters, OR, © 1991). Used by permission.

"Is It the Truth?" by Leslie E. Duncan, quoted from *HomeLife* magazine, March 1997.

"Running Late" from *The Signature of Jesus* by Brennan Manning (Multnomah Publishers, Inc., Sisters, OR, © 1992). Used by permission.

"The Test" from *Don't Count the Days, Make the Days Count* by Ed Agresta.

"Learning from a Mother's Tenderness" by Charles Swindoll from *Growing Wise in Family Life,* Charles Swindoll, copyright © 1988 (Word Publishing, Nashville, TN). All rights reserved.

"Asking for Forgiveness" by Luis Palau, adapted from *Calling America and the Nations to Christ* by Luis Palau, © 1994 by Luis Palau (Thomas Nelson Publishers, Nashville, TN). Luis Palau speaks to millions of people around the world, has three daily radio programs broadcast on more than 570 stations in 25 countries, and is the best-selling author of *God Is Relevant* (Doubleday) and *What Is a Real Christian?* (published in 32 languages worldwide). Used by permission. Luis Palau is the president of the Luis Palau Evangelistic Association, P.O. Box 1173, Portland, OR 97207, http://www.lpea.org, lpea@palau.org.

"Three Red Marbles," author unknown.

"Tommy" from *The Light Behind the Star* by David R. Johnson (Multnomah Publishers, Inc., Sisters, OR, © 1989). Used by permission of the author. David R. Johnson is now retired after 28 years with the San Jose Police Department. David can now pursue more fully his love of writing. He can be contacted at P.O. Box 18661, San Jose, CA 95158. To God be the glory!

"Advice" by Billy Graham. Quoted from *The Christian Reader* magazine. Original source unknown.

"The Admonition Suit" from *Home Town Tales* by Philip Gulley (Multnomah Publishers, Inc., Sisters, OR, © 1998). Used by permission.

LOVE

"Ben and Virginia" by Gwyn Williams, freelance writer, Huntsville, AL. Used by permission.

"In a Cathedral of Fence Posts and Harleys" by Neil Parker, freelance writer, Burnaby, British Columbia, Canada. Used by permission of the author.

"Mistaken Identity" by Edward C. Boland. Quoted from *The Christian Reader,* September/October 1995.

"The Gold Box" by James C. Dobson from *Home with a Heart,* copyright © 1996 James C. Dobson. Used by permission of the author.

"The Portrait" from *The Ten(der) Commandments* by Ron Mehl (Multnomah Publishers, Inc., Sisters, OR, © 1998). Used by permission.

"For Richer or Poorer" retold by Rochelle M. Pennington, newspaper columnist; contributing author to *Stories for the Heart, Chicken Soup for the Soul, and Life's Little Instruction Book;* and coauthor of *Highlighted in Yellow.* You may reach her at N1911 Double D. Rd., Campbellsport, WI 53010; (920)533-5880. Used by permission.

"The Color of Love" by Allison Harms, freelance writer, Lake Oswego, OR. Used by permission.

"Roses" by Dr. Steve Stephens, freelance writer, Clackamas, OR. Used by permission.

"Close Call" by Patricia Beecher. Quoted from *The Christian Reader,* March/April 1997.

"Simple Wooden Boxes" by Martha Pendergrass Templeton, freelance writer, Mentone, AL. Used by permission.

"Politely Partisan" by Lois Wyse, from *You Wouldn't Believe What My Grandchild Did...* (Simon & Schuster, © 1994).

"Romance" taken from FIT TO BE TIED by Bill & Lynne Hybels. Copyright © 1991 by Bill & Lynne Hybels. Used by permission of Zondervan Publishing House.

"In the Trenches" from *Locking Arms* by Stu Weber (Multnomah Publishers, Inc., Sisters, OR, © 1995). Used by permission.

"A Million, Million" by Debi Stack, freelance writer, Kansas City, MO. Used by permission.

"Twenty Ways to Make Your Wife Feel Special" by Al Gray. Used by permission of the author.

"The Eyes of the Heart" by Luci Swindoll taken from WE BRAKE FOR JOY! by Patsy Clairmont, Barbara Johnson, Marilyn Meberg, Luci Swindoll, Sheila Walsh, and Thelma Wells. Copyright © 1998 by Women of Faith, Inc. Used by permission of Zondervan Publishing House.

"The One the Father Loves the Most" from *Lion and Lamb* by

MOTIVATION

1224 (worldwide). FAX: 973-227-9742 (US/CANADA) or (+1 973)227-9742 (worldwide). E-mail: info@epinc.com Web site: www.epinc.com.

"Two Diaries" from *The Legacy* by Steven J. Lawson (Multnomah Publishers, Inc., Sisters, OR, © 1998).

"The Negative Neighbor" by Charles Swindoll from *Three Steps Forward, Two Steps Back,* Charles Swindoll, copyright © 1983 (Word Publishing, Nashville, TN). All rights reserved.

ENCOURAGEMENT

"Every Minute" by Cecil G. Osborne, quoted from *God's Little Instruction Book for Dad* (Honor Books, Inc., Tulsa, OK, © 1994).

"Coming Home" by David Redding, from *Jesus Makes Me Laugh* © 1977 by David Redding (Zondervan Publishing House, Grand Rapids, MI.). Used with permission of the author. Dr. David A. Redding is Senior Minister of Liberty Presbyterian Church, Delaware, Ohio, and the author of 24 books including his latest *A Rose Will Grow Anywhere* which is available through Starborne House, P.O. Box 767, Delaware, OH 43015.

"Jimmy Durante" by Tim Hansel from *Holy Sweat,* Tim Hansel, copyright © 1987 (Word Publishing, Nashville, TN). All rights reserved.

"Our Friendship Tree" by Harrison Kelly, freelance writer, living in Memphis, TN, with his wife and their two children, Brad and Kristina. His credits include *2nd Helping of Chicken Soup for the Woman's Soul.*

"The Policeman and the Towels" taken from SIMPLE WONDERS by Christopher de Vinck. Copyright © 1995 by Christopher de Vinck. Used by permission of Zondervan Publishing House.

"Costly Error" as cited in *More of...The Best of Bits and Pieces,* Rob Gilbert, ed. *More of...The Best of Bits and Pieces* is copyrighted © 1997 by The Economics Press, Inc., 12 Daniel Road, Fairfield, NJ 07004-2565 USA; Phone: 800-526-2554 (US/CANADA) or (+1 973)227-1224 (worldwide). FAX: 973-227-9742 (US/CANADA) or (+1 973)227-9742 (worldwide). E-mail: info@epinc.com Web site: www.epinc.com.

"An Important Lesson" by Rabbi Harold S. Kushner quoted from *A Cup of Coffee at the Soul Cafe.* Copyright © 1998 (Leonard Sweet; Broadman and Holman Publishers, Nashville, TN).

"Encouraging Words" by Barbara Johnson taken from WE BRAKE

FATHERHOOD

SPORTS

"Unexpected Places" by Rochelle M. Pennington, newspaper columnist; contributing author to *Stories for the Heart, Chicken Soup for the Soul,* and *Life's Little Instruction Book;* and coauthor of *Highlighted in Yellow.* You may reach Rochelle at N1911 Double D. Rd., Campbellsport, WI 53010; (920)533-5880. Used by permission.

"Caught Any Yet?" by Helen F. Duplayee. Reprinted with permission from the May 1998 *Reader's Digest.* © 1998 by The Reader's Digest Association.

"Releasing the Arrow" from *Tender Warrior* by Stu Weber (Multnomah Publishers, Inc., Sisters, OR, © 1993). Used by permission.

"Confessions to a Bench Coach" by Vickey L. Banks. Used by permission. Vickey Banks is an inspirational speaker and writer with a passion to help others experience a dynamic and intimate walk with God. You can contact Vickey at 405/728-2305.

"Integrity" by Denis Waitley from *Being the Best,* copyright © (Thomas Nelson, Inc., Nashville, TN). Used by permission.

LEGACY

"A Splendid Torch" by George Bernard Shaw quoted from *Strength for a Man's Heart,* edited by Paul C. Brownlow (Brownlow Publishing Company, Inc., Fort Worth, TX 76117, ©1997).

"A Single Crocus" From WHERE WONDERS PREVAIL by Joan Wester Anderson. Copyright © 1996 by Joan Wester Anderson. Reprinted by permission of Ballantine Books, a Division of Random House, Inc. Reprinted with permission of The Reader's Digest Association.

"Dad's Mark" by Bill Hybels. Taken from HONEST TO GOD? by Bill Hybels. Copyright © 1990 by Bill Hybels. Used by permission of Zondervan Publishing House.

"Exchanging Gifts" by Cathy Downs, freelance writer, Caser, NC, from *The Reading Teacher,* Vol. 48, No. 2, October 1994 (The International Reading Association, Newark, DE). Used by permission.

"Doing What Our Father Says" by Luis Palau from *Devotions #2.* Used by permission. Copyright © Luis Palau, who speaks to millions of people around the world, has three daily radio programs broadcast on more than 570 stations in 25 countries, and is the best-selling author of *God Is*

Relevant (Doubleday) and *What Is a Real Christian?* (published in 32 languages worldwide). Luis Palau is the president of the Luis Palau Evangelistic Association, P.O. Box 1173, Portland, OR 97207, http://www.lpea.org, lpea@palau.org.

"Between the Lines" by Charlotte Adelsperger, freelance writer, Overland Park, KS. Used by permission.

"What You Remember Most" from *The Legacy* by Steven J. Lawson (Multnomah Publishers, Inc., Sisters, OR, © 1998). Used by permission.

"Legacy of Love" by Jane Landin Ramirez, freelance writer, Lubbock, TX. Quoted from *It's Just About Christmas* (Christianity Today, Inc.). Used by permission of the author.

"The Power of Being There" by Thom Hunter from *Those Not-So-Still Small Voices*. Used by permission. Thom Hunter is an author and speaker on Christian family life, bringing humor to reality. His books include *Those Not-So-Still Small Voices* and *Like Father, Like Sons...and Daughter, Too.* Thom and Lisa have five children: Zach, 20; Russell, 18; Donovan, 17; Patrick, 15 and Lauren, 12. They live in Norman, Oklahoma. Contact Thom at 405-329-6773, or e-mail at TH2950@sbc.com. Reprinted with permission from the April 1995 *Reader's Digest*.

"Memories" by Dennis Rainey quoted from *Pulling Weeds, Planting Seeds*. Copyright © 1989 Dennis Rainey, freelance writer and executive director of Family Life, Little Rock, AR. Used by permission.

"Purpose and Destiny" by Francis of Assisi. Quoted from *The Signature of Jesus* by Brennan Manning (Multnomah Publishers, Inc., Sisters, OR, © 1992).

"My Dad" by Charles Swindoll. Taken from COME BEFORE WINTER by Charles Swindoll. Copyright © 1985 by Charles R. Swindoll, Inc. Used by permission of Zondervan Publishing House.

"Just Enough Time" by Barbara Baumgardner, freelance writer, Bend, OR. Used by permission of the author. From *Moody*, June 1991.

"What a Heart" by the children of Dick Wimer. Quoted from his memorial service bulletin.

"A Father's Blessing" by Morgan Cryar. This article was taken from *Decision* magazine. Copyright © 1998 Billy Graham Evangelistic Association. Used by permission. All rights reserved. Morgan Cryar, a recording artist with Damascus Road Records, lives in Hermitage, TN with his wife and six (soon to be seven) children. In addition to his concert ministry, he is in demand as a marriage and family speaker. For information, contact: Morgan Cryar at 615-884-9530.

FAITH

"Worry" by Billy Graham from *Unto the Hills,* Billy Graham, copyright © 1996 (Word Publishing, Nashville, TN). All rights reserved.

"A Perfect Mistake" by Cheryl Walterman Stewart, freelance writer, Arlington, TX. Used by permission.

"When God Takes Your Hand" condensed from *God Works the Night Shift* by Ron Mehl (Multnomah Publishers, Inc., Sisters, OR, © 1994). Used by permission.

"Planning Ahead" from *That I May Know God* by Kenneth Boa (Multnomah Publishers, Inc., Sisters, OR, © 1998).

"Peace" by Billy Graham from *Unto the Hills,* Billy Graham, copyright ©1996 (Word Publishing, Nashville, TN). All rights reserved.

"The Oak Tree" from *No Wonder They Call Him the Savior* by Max Lucado (Multnomah Publishers, Inc., Sisters, OR, © 1986). Used by permission.

"Don't Give Up" by Morris Chalfant, freelance writer, Kankakee, IL. Used by permission.

"Just a Kid with Cerebral Palsy" by Tony Campolo quoted from *U,* April/May 1998.

"Even If It's Dark" from *God Works the Night Shift* by Ron Mehl (Multnomah Publishers, Inc., Sisters, OR, © 1994). Used by permission.

"Traveling Through" by Billy Graham from *Hope for the Troubled Heart.*

"Tommy's Daddies" by Casandra Lindell, freelance writer, Portland, OR. Used by permission.

"Learning 'bout Prayer" from *Standing Together* by Howard Hendricks (Multnomah Publishers, Inc., Sisters, OR, © 1995). Used by permission.

"Two Prayers" by Andrew Gillies, 1870-1942. Quoted from *Masterpiece of Religious Verse,* edited by James Dalton Morrison, New York: Harper and Brothers Publishers, © 1948.

"The Bootblack and the Ph.D." by Ruth Graham, quoted from *Legacy of a Pack Rat* (Thomas Nelson Publishers, Nashville, TN, © 1989). Used with permission of the author.

"Thinking of Life" from *The Light Behind the Star* by David R. Johnson (Multnomah Publishers, Inc., Sisters, OR, © 1989). Used by permission of the author. David R. Johnson is now retired after 28 years with the San Jose Police Department. David can now pursue more fully his love of writing. He can be contacted at P.O. Box 18661, San Jose, CA 95158. To God be the glory!

"Right on Time" from *Surprise Endings* by Ron Mehl (Multnomah Publishers, Inc., Sisters, OR, © 1993). Used by permission.

"The Final Glance" from *Six Hours One Friday* by Max Lucado (Multnomah Publishers, Inc., Sisters, OR, © 1989). Used by permission.